GREAT BRAND STORIES ARSENAL

Winning together: The story of the Arsenal brand

John Simmons and Matt Simmons

CYANBOOKS

Copyright © 2006 John Simmons and Matt Simmons

First published in 2006 by Cyan Books, an imprint of

Cyan Communications Limited
119 Wardour Street
London W1F 0UW
United Kingdom
T: +44 (0)20 7565 6120
E: sales@cyanbooks.com
www.cyanbooks.com

A CIP record for this book is available from the British Library

ISBN 1-904879-60-8

Book design: Jon Lee

Picture credits: Arsenal (pages 52–3 and 105); EMPICS (pages 11, 19, 30, 33, 40, 41, 47, 49, 57, 60–61, 65, 68–9, 73, 78–9, 83, 90–91, 94–5, 103, 120, 134–5, 148, 151, 159, 162, 168, 171 and 190–91); Jon Lee (pages 6–7 and 144–5); Tom Lynham (page 137); Dan McAlister (pages 112–13); Jessie Simmons/Full Stop Photography (pages 14, 17, 22–3, 34–5, 36, 108, 111, 124–5, 129, 154–5, 174–5, 181, 183, 184–5 and 192)

Printed and bound in Great Britain

CONTENTS

THANK YOU

This book, even more than most, was informed and shaped by conversation. Conversations with each other, conversations with players, writers and designers, and, most importantly, conversations with other Arsenal fans. Our first thank you then is to all Arsenal fans. It is no exaggeration to say that this book could not exist without you.

A number of conversations are reproduced within the book, and we would particularly like to thank Frank McLintock, Pat Rice, Alex Fynn, Ben Evans, John Sorrell, Kevin Whitcher and Nick Liddell for their time and insights. Ian Ridley, Amy Lawrence and Andy Milligan also helped. Jon Lee provided us with stimulating conversation over a drink or two, and more importantly, designed this book.

Martin Liu and Pom Somkabcharti of Cyan Books gave us great support. Other books were invaluable too and we have tried our best to acknowledge them fully where extracts appear in the text, and we are grateful to the authors: *Wenger: The making of a legend* by Jasper Rees; *The Glorious Game: Extra time* by Alex Fynn and Kevin Whitcher; *Addicted* by Tony Adams; *The Beautiful Game* by David Conn. The website www.arsenal-world.co.uk remains a daily source of useful information, and *The Gooner* is not to be missed. We would also like to thank Jon Spurling, whom we haven't met, but whose excellent alternative history of Arsenal, *Rebels for the Cause* was a fascinating and useful companion while writing.

Finally we would like to thank a couple of Arsenal fans we do know – Jessie, who took many of the pictures, and Linda, who provided support, tea and typing.

DEDICATION

This book is dedicated to the Arsenal Stadium, Highbury, and all those who stood, sat, won, lost, clapped and sang there.

1913–2006

"A club should be like a great big family
with all members of it sticking and
pulling together in the same direction."
Herbert Chapman

We started writing this chapter by email, sending each other pieces and then responding, from John to Matt and back again.

John

From: John Simmons
To: Matt Simmons
Subject: A game of two halves

From father to son, from generation to generation. Many people will be shocked, or think I'm being frivolous, when I say that the thing I was always keenest to pass on to you was a love of the Arsenal. But that's the truth. I'm sure it was the same for my father. And the fact that your sister Jessie is Arsenal through and through doubles my delight and relief.

Supporting the Arsenal is a family tradition. We have fewer of these traditions today as political, social and religious allegiances are much looser. It seems, though, to have had the effect of strengthening sporting allegiances, perhaps to fill some of the gap. There is something political, social and religious in our adherence to Arsenal. Watching Arsenal play, in a large and like-minded crowd, is one way to express a belief in a world without barriers of race and class. So we associate ourselves with these people wearing the team colours, on and off the pitch, we share the values; it's a big family in which our family is an integral part of the whole. It's in the blood, we share the DNA, we can never lose the sense of belonging to this family.

That's an incredibly valuable quality for any brand to have. There's probably no other area of commercial life where loyalty runs so deep. Other brands have to work hard to provide emotional connections and memories; here we have a constant stream. What's your first memory of the Arsenal?

Matt

From: Matt Simmons
To: John Simmons
Subject: A game of two halves

My first Arsenal memory. October, 1982, Birmingham City at home. I remember practically nothing from the game, a fact which has less to do with a failing memory, and more to do with the fact that I don't think I was paying much attention at the time. Now, in my defence the game was a boring 0–0 draw, an experience which at least prepared me for the last few years of George Graham's reign at Highbury. I never travelled to Highbury in the expectation of seeing fluent, exciting (or even competent) football. Obviously that all changed with Arsène Wenger. But in early eighties North London, Arsenal were far from being a fashionable team. On the other hand, Spurs at the time were an exciting, skilful side, containing exotic, foreign internationals, and still capable of winning the odd trophy...

So, tragically, my first memory of watching a whole match was the 1981 FA Cup final replay between Spurs and Manchester City on the telly. Though I remember greatly enjoying it, I also remember being aware that this Spurs team who had won the game were not my team, in fact were the opposite. For reasons I couldn't begin to understand, let alone explain, Spurs were the enemy of my team Arsenal.

Anyway, back to October 1982. The game was terrible, but even if it had been a 5–4 thriller I might well not remember much about it. At that stage it was less about the football, and more about the whole experience of going to the Arsenal with my Dad. You're quite right to stress the importance of the family tradition to football. I grew to love and understand football, and Arsenal, but initially I just think I enjoyed it as a chance to bond with you. I haven't discussed this with Jessie, but I suspect it might have been the same for her. Jessie started coming with us a couple of years later, and I remember that at first she was more interested in us, and the crowd, than the game taking place. That changed of course, just as it had for me previously.

We left the ground after the Birmingham game, and joined the long queue outside Arsenal station. Just the same as everyone around us, you wanted to conduct an inquest into the game. However, upon mentioning some of the (few) significant events from the game it soon became obvious to you that I hadn't been paying much attention. Drastic measures were obviously called for, leading to you issuing the threat that if, when we next came, I couldn't tell you what had happened on the pitch, we wouldn't be coming again.

The threat worked. I've barely taken my eyes off the pitch in all the years since. What a day. My first Arsenal game, and an early introduction to the concept of tough love...

John

From: John Simmons
To: Matt Simmons
Subject: A game of two halves

You mentioned a 5–4 thriller. I suspect that's because I've talked often about the game at Highbury in February 1958 when Manchester United beat Arsenal 5–4. This was the game that infected me with a lifelong passion for football and – despite the defeat – for Arsenal.

At the time Manchester United were definitely the glamorous team. They were known as the Busby Babes because the team was filled with young (mainly teenage) players. They had Duncan Edwards at half-back, idolised as the finest prospect of his generation, and a young Bobby Charlton. They played with style, swagger and a youthful joy. Of course, I hated them, because they weren't my team. My team played in red shirts with white sleeves and was full of older players with Brylcreemed hair, including my favourite player Derek Tapscott (Tappy). By any objective assessment, I should have supported the Busby Babes. But objectivity rarely comes into it when it's about supporting a football team – or a brand.

My dad took me from home (near King's Cross) by tube. You could feel the excitement in the air as you walked along the street, but it was that walk up from the platform of Arsenal station that burned into my memory as a 'brand experience'. A noisy hubbub, not a lot of singing (that came later in the sixties) but loud talking, shouting and the noise of horns and rattles. Inside the ground we made our way to our usual spot on the North Bank, the second barrier back, behind the goal. When I was smaller I sat on the barrier, on a cushion, with my dad behind me, holding me on. But by this age, nearly ten, I was standing on a stool. My dad came prepared.

29th September 1956
Division One – Arsenal v Manchester United
Arsenal's Derek Tapscott cries out in frustration after his shot beat
Manchester United goalkeeper Ray Wood but missed the goal

The match started, the noise was amazing, but the situation on the pitch couldn't have been worse. The United youngsters swept forward at pace, making the Arsenal players look leaden-footed. By half-time we were 3–0 down and it was a gloomy cup of tea we shared. But the second half brought a transformation. Arsenal equalised, 3–3, and it seemed as if the crowd had roared them back into the game. Then it slipped away again, we went 5–3 down before my hero Tappy scored to make it 5–4. We lost but the Arsenal had won my devotion for life. It was a performance full of character and I was proud of them. You don't always have to win. You associate yourself with the effort, the commitment, the dreams that you see out on the pitch.

A few days later it was all put in perspective, not that I was mature enough to see it that way at the time. Manchester United had a midweek European match against Red Star Belgrade and their plane crashed on the runway at Munich Airport. Eight players died including Duncan Edwards and most of the team that I had seen three days earlier. Their manager Matt Busby almost lost his life. Strangely, it was the making of the Manchester United legend. For Arsenal, though, the bleak years of unglamorous underachievement were to continue. But there was still something there that made us the Arsenal. I'm interested in trying to define what that is because it's nothing to do with style of football.

Matt

From: Matt Simmons
To: John Simmons
Subject: A game of two halves

You're quite right to say it's nothing to do with the style of football, as I'm sure the fans of most other clubs would be the first to point out.

I wonder how central the actual football is to any club's identity though. Our great rivals, Spurs, are a good example of a club who have positioned the idea of playing football the 'right' way centrally to their identity. But, as you know, this aspect of their identity is a relatively recent development, springing from Bill Nicholson's great side of the early sixties. Furthermore, Spurs haven't been known for their stylish football for some years now (even appointing our very own George Graham as manager at one point!), yet this has had very little impact on Spurs fans' sense of identity. The football seems (almost) incidental.

It would be easy to say that actually there is very little to differentiate one club's identity from another's. I think this would be wrong though. Every club, and Arsenal more than most, has its own 'feel', something quite distinct from the shirts the players wear, the manager at the time, or even the ground the club play at.

For myself, this sense of identity seems to sit more with the fans, than with the club itself. Our fans are often criticised for being too quiet at games, something which has led to our (current) ground being re-christened "The Highbury Library" by rival fans. On the other hand, there's a lot to be proud of. In over twenty years of going to Highbury I've rarely, if ever, heard racial abuse. We have one of the most cosmopolitan and tolerant crowds in the country. There is practically no hooligan problem among Arsenal fans, and most (unfortunately not all) of our fans support the club with humour and passion. There's a certain bleak sense of humour that comes with supporting Arsenal, that you just don't find amongst fans of other big clubs. We always seem to expect the worst, even at the best of times.

Ultimately, as AFC Wimbledon have shown, a club's identity rests with the fans.

The famous entrance to the marble halls

John

From: John Simmons
To: Matt Simmons
Subject: A game of two halves

I believe identification starts at a local level, and locality is the strongest element of a football club's identity. Arsenal overcame the strongest threat to its identity when it switched location from Woolwich in south London (where it was the 'works team' for the Woolwich Arsenal) to Highbury in north London at the time of the First World War. So within the memory of any current Arsenal fan the club has always been based in this area of north London.

That's why the relocation of the ground from Highbury in recent years has been such an emotive issue. From a purely financial point of view Arsenal should have moved to a new stadium on the outskirts of London. Most things would have been easier: no problems with planning permission, much lower costs, parking for all. But you cannot leave these decisions solely to the accountants and the Arsenal board at least understood the central importance of the local association to the Arsenal brand. So the move is less than a mile down the road, despite all the logistical and financial complications involved. It was a brand-driven decision and one that the board got right.

I say that almost with surprise because football club directors don't always show such awareness and, particularly in recent years, they tend to see only currency symbols in front of their eyes when considering their brand assets. Looking objectively at the brand situation the big clubs have moved beyond purely local identification to a national and international level. It's been a joke for many years that Manchester United fans come from Torquay and Yarmouth, Singapore and Sydney, rather than from Manchester. And this is when the figures start to be most seductive for a football director, because you can sell TV rights and merchandise to people all around the world as well as all around the country.

Arsenal is a less nationally spread brand; our most loyal fans still come from north London, but there is no doubt that this is changing. But perhaps it's not changing as fast as the international dimension. Arsenal is now a brand that people throughout the world identify with; it's a cosmopolitan brand with strong roots in a local community. If you think about other global brands that's not surprising. Starbucks from Seattle, Ben & Jerry's from Vermont, Guinness from Dublin – brands can use the story of their local roots to add depth and emotional resonance to the way they are perceived.

Matt

From: Matt Simmons
To: John Simmons
Subject: A game of two halves

There's no doubt that this sense of local identification is enormously important to Arsenal's (and most clubs') sense of identity. Most genuine football fans would agree that when it comes to determining who you support there are only really two factors that come in to play: who your family's team is, and who your local team is.

Luckily for both of us, Arsenal were both our family and local team. I've often wondered though what it must be like to be a born and bred Arsenal fan, but grow up in a different part of the country. Imagine, for example, growing up in Manchester or Liverpool supporting Arsenal, going to Highbury for a game and hearing a large part of the crowd chanting "you dirty northern bastards" at the opposition. Where would your loyalties lie?

As you say, the majority of our support does still come from London and the surrounding area, but our largest growth area is international. Any regular at Highbury is now used to the hundreds

A local North London street sign, locally adapted

of Scandinavian and Japanese fans who attend games every week. The Arsenal website, arsenal.com, is available in Japanese as well as English. What is it that attracts these fans to Arsenal?

Any brand's local roots are an important part of its image, but is this what attracts a fan in Osaka or Stockholm to Arsenal?

I think, inevitably, that this will be of lesser importance to an international fan, than a local fan. Does someone from thousands of miles away care whether Arsenal play at Ashburton Grove or just outside the M25? Possibly not. For these fans I think the history and prestige of the club, its iconic players and the style of play will be more important than where they play.

Part of the challenge for Arsenal, and any big club, is keeping these different sets of supporters, who may want very different things, happy. So far Arsenal have managed this fairly well. It's a fine balancing act to maintain though, to retain and look after your core support, whilst also building the club as an international brand.

John

___

From: John Simmons
To: Matt Simmons
Subject: A game of two halves

There's another aspect of internationalism that has become more important over the last decade. When Dennis Bergkamp signed for Arsenal in 1996 he was the first foreign superstar to join the club. English football had a deep suspicion of foreign players until the Premier League came into being in 1992. Before then the conventional wisdom of the British managers had been that the sight of a muddy pitch on a wet winter's day would drain colour from the faces and spirit from the beings of any player not born in the UK.

Things are different now, and they're much better for being different. Players like the French Eric Cantona for Manchester United, the Italian Gianfranco Zola for Chelsea and the Dutch Dennis Bergkamp for Arsenal were pioneers in changing the perceptions of British football fans. Now at Arsenal we have loved Vieira, Henry and Pires primarily because they're great footballers – but also because we like their sophisticated edge, the *je ne sais quoi* that their Frenchness adds to the Arsenal image. And, of course, having a French manager in Arsène Wenger has been a triumph. He is a brand ambassador whom we feel proud of because he represents the Arsenal tradition with a modern, cosmopolitan twist. The important thing is that he is a winner, but a winner who knows the ways of a world beyond these narrow shores.

This internationalism is under some threat, however. If UEFA gets its way (with the support of all the national associations) there will be a limit on the number of foreign players in a first team squad. This will put more emphasis on clubs developing players within their youth academies. David Dein, Arsenal's influential vice-chairman, was ahead of the game when he appointed Liam Brady in 1996 to head the youth academy and stated that it was "the most important

Dennis Bergkamp

job in the club". Young players are now coming through to the first team squad in quantity and quality. But these players are not necessarily local boys. Arsenal's teenage reserves were born in Italy, Switzerland, Ivory Coast, Denmark, all over the world. Whatever UEFA might wish, it won't be feasible (or desirable for the fans) to hold back the international tide.

Being based in London, perhaps the world's most cosmopolitan city, gives Arsenal a brand advantage. It helps to attract high-quality players, whether the 15-year-old with potential or the 25-year-old established star. And the cosmopolitan result, the mixing of nations, helps to promote the brand in markets all around the world.

Matt

From: Matt Simmons
To: John Simmons
Subject: A game of two halves

There can be no doubt that Arsenal's location in London is of enormous value to the club, and the brand. Foreign players angling for a move to the Premiership frequently comment upon their desire to live and work in London. In addition, it is far easier for foreign players to settle in London, where immigrant communities from practically every country in the world already exist, than in say Newcastle or Middlesbrough.

This is also reflected amongst Arsenal's supporters. Arsenal have the highest percentage of season ticket holders from ethnic minorities of any club in the Premiership. The 2002 Premier League fan survey found that 7.7% of Arsenal's season ticket holders described themselves as outside the white British category, compared with a national average of less than 1%. Given the multicultural nature of North London, Arsenal should actually have even more supporters from ethnic minorities than they do, but nonetheless it is an encouraging start.

Of course, things could have been very different. As most Arsenal fans know, and as Spurs fans frequently remind us, Arsenal weren't even originally a North London club. Without the move north our local rivals would now be Charlton and Millwall. It's impossible to predict what else would now be different, but it's hard to believe Arsenal would have enjoyed the same level of success without the move. Henry Norris, the driving force behind the re-location certainly understood this. For better or worse Norris was a man ahead of his time, and together with Herbert Chapman, is largely responsible for the club we know and love today.

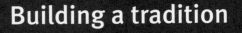

Building a tradition

"I'm quite happy to wear a different shirt next season, so bring it on and let's add another chapter to that old tradition we're so fond of and that draws us towards that magnificent club in the first place."
Highbury Spy, Gooner fanzine, January 2005

Arsenal's image is founded in its history, and the fans have been just as keen to maintain this image as the club. As Arsenal fans sing to their Chelsea counterparts in these post-Abramovich times: "You still ain't got no history." Even Chelsea winning trophies does not change the thought; the presumption remains that Chelsea is a club built on sand.

By contrast, Arsenal's history is long and glorious, both on and off the pitch. The Bank of England club, who were the first to install under-soil heating, and were powerful and prestigious enough to get a tube station re-named after themselves; even in times when Arsenal's success on the pitch has dried up the fans could always feel pride in what the club represented. Yet, as fans of other clubs frequently point out, Arsenal's history isn't without its shady side, and Arsenal have never been in any danger of winning popularity contests among neutral supporters.

The truth lies somewhere between these two opposing views. The good and the bad have often co-existed at Arsenal, as they have at any club, indeed in any large organisation. Consider almost any of the world's leading brands, and you will struggle to find one whose story isn't troubled at some point by controversy, in many cases of a far more serious nature than that surrounding Arsenal.

Of course, none of the darker side of Arsenal's history forms any part of its brand identity today. This is only to be expected, yet Arsenal would not have been so successful, would not be in as strong a position today if they had always played strictly by the rules.

Arsenal were first formed in 1886, but the club formed then would be completely unrecognisable to anyone today. The exact origins of the club remain somewhat obscure, as there were several works teams at the Woolwich Arsenal who contributed players to the team that would become Arsenal. The most significant of these works teams was called Dial Square, and it was under this name that the club played their first ever match, against Eastern Wanderers in December 1886. Two Scots, John Humble and David Danskin, became the driving force behind the club in those early days. They were both workers at the Woolwich Arsenal, and in the early days at least, both regularly played for Royal Arsenal, as the club became known shortly after playing its first game. Danskin was responsible for founding the club, and raising the funds to support it, while in 1891 it was Humble who proposed that Royal Arsenal should turn professional. It was also at this same AGM in 1891 that the club changed its name to Woolwich Arsenal. By this time Arsenal were already playing in red shirts, due to the generous donation of a full set of kits by Nottingham Forest; the famous white sleeves weren't actually added until Herbert Chapman's reign at the club.

This decision to turn professional sparked the first of many controversial episodes in Arsenal's history. At this time the London FA were fiercely opposed to professionalism within the sport (some would say that the current English FA still maintain an admirably amateurish approach to football) and so immediately banned Arsenal from taking part in any of its competitions. For two years the club searched for a solution, whilst having only FA Cup matches left to give them competitive football. This wasn't much of a consolation, as Woolwich Arsenal were thrashed in the first round of the competition in both of these years. In 1893 the Football League Second Division was expanded from 12 to 15 clubs, and Arsenal were duly elected to the League, the first London-based club to do so.

This, though, was far from being the start of Arsenal's success story. They still had no ground of their own (between 1886 and 1913 they played in a number of different locations in and around Plumstead), were a fairly mediocre Second Division side, and were already, at this early point in their history, becoming unpopular with other clubs. This quote, from the *Derby Post*, seems to sum up the attitude of many visitors to the club at this time. One of the Derby chaps was heard to mutter that:

"A journey to the molten interior of the earth's core would be rather more pleasant and comfortable an experience than our

forthcoming visit to the Royal Arsenal."

Derby Post, 15 January 1891

This feeling persisted throughout the 1890s, and was based not only in the difficulties inherent in getting to Woolwich Arsenal, but also in the club's uncompromising and rugged playing style. This image of Arsenal as a dirty, boring or lucky team has persisted ever since, though no-one would describe Arsène Wenger's Arsenal as boring. Arsenal's status as a dirty team is still frequently debated throughout the media, who have never seemed able to grant Arsenal the kind of respect and affection directed towards the other giants of the English game, Manchester United and Liverpool.

Although Arsenal may not have done much to endear themselves to anyone during the early part of their history, the next twenty years at the club were fairly uneventful, and certainly unsuccessful. It was the arrival of Henry Norris in 1910 that was to cement Arsenal's position as London's most hated club, as well as building the foundations of the modern Arsenal.

Norris was a self-made millionaire, blunt, outspoken and used to getting his way. Norris would have fitted in perfectly as a club chairman in the modern era, though it is unlikely that many chairmen now have even heard of him. His first action upon taking over the club was to propose a merger between Woolwich Arsenal and Fulham, where he was also a director. It was only after the League turned down this proposal that Norris moved to carry out the most significant action in Arsenal's history. The League suggested that there was an obvious conflict of interest in Norris having control over two clubs, and that he should divest himself of his interest in one of them. Norris decided to stick with Woolwich Arsenal, though he also decided that something would have to change. Woolwich Arsenal was no more, and Arsenal Football Club was born.

When Norris took over Woolwich Arsenal they were a poorly supported team, on the verge of bankruptcy. If they were ever to succeed Norris decided that they would have to move to an area with a larger potential fan base and good transport links. To modern fans the parallels with the case of the Milton Keynes Dons are clear, and certainly Norris's actions were unpopular with Woolwich Arsenal's fans, as well as the other clubs whose catchment areas he was potentially infringing on. At this time there was nothing in the rules to say that Norris had to ask for the League's permission to move, which was just as well, as the League didn't approve either.

Norris looked at a number of sites in North and West London, before settling upon Highbury, which at the time was home to St John's College of Divinity. Ignoring all objections, Norris signed the deeds, and spent a small fortune on transforming Highbury into a football ground. The first match at Highbury (which Arsenal won 2–1, beating Leicester Fosse) took place on the 6th September 1913.

Unfortunately, by this point Arsenal were no longer a First Division club. Relegated in 1913, their last season before moving to Highbury, the club set an unwanted record. The 1912–13 season saw Arsenal record the lowest number of goals, wins and points ever by a First Division club. Thus the 1913–14 season saw Arsenal not only in a new home, but in a new division.

The start of the First World War in 1914 rendered football largely irrelevant for the next four years, and the league programme did not resume until September 1919. In the last season (1914–15) to be completed before the suspension of the league, Arsenal had finished fifth, two places lower than they had managed in the previous season. Despite Norris's massive investment in the club, they would still have to start in the Second Division. It was at this point that Norris carried out the act which, above everything else, guaranteed him lasting infamy. As all Arsenal fans know, the club's officials are masters of understatement, always eager to avoid the slightest hint of controversy. Yet even the official history of Arsenal can't ignore Norris's actions in 1919, referring to them as:

"The single most outrageous enterprise ever conceived in the history of English football."

(p. 42, *The Official History*)

Details are scarce as to what exactly happened. Only the eventual outcome is clear – Arsenal began season 1919–20 in Division One. The decision had been taken to expand the First Division from 20 to 22 clubs, and whenever the division had been expanded previously the top clubs from the Second Division were promoted, while the bottom clubs from the First Division were automatically re-elected. This was not to happen in 1919 however. Instead, Norris used the League's 1919 Annual General Meeting to convince his fellow directors that Arsenal should be elected to the newly expanded First Division at the expense of the club who finished 20th in the 1914–15 season. It is a source of continuing, if admittedly perverse, delight to many Arsenal fans that the unfortunate club finishing in 20th was Spurs. All brands, to some extent, define themselves by comparison to what they are not. Apple is not IBM, Pepsi is not Coke. Here Henry Norris, having already encroached on their North London territory, clearly defined Arsenal as definitely not Spurs.

Henry Norris had been elected a Tory MP in 1918, and he used all of his influence and political savvy to ensure Arsenal's promotion. He secretly canvassed all of his fellow directors in order to convince them of the worth of Arsenal's case, and was able to secure the support of the League President, John Mckenna, who was also the owner of Liverpool. Only one club was not included in Norris's canvassing: Spurs. Norris was even careful to ensure the support of Chelsea, who had finished 19th in 1914–15, usually a relegation position. Chelsea were re-elected to the First Division without a vote, a proposal put forward by Norris's ally, John Mckenna. In this way, Spurs were isolated from any potential allies, and their fate was sealed.

Obviously the events above did nothing to improve Arsenal's relationship with Spurs, or indeed anyone else. Already far from being a universally loved club, Arsenal became widely despised. The events of 1919 are not as widely known as they once were, but among the more hardcore elements of Spurs fanbase they still provide additional motivation to hate Arsenal. Even Chelsea fans, whose club benefited from, and were complicit with, Norris's actions, continue to refer to Arsenal's shady past, as this passage taken from the Chelsea fansite Blueandwhitearmy shows:

"Us Chelsea supporters feel that there is something profoundly rotten about Arsenal FC. We usually attribute it to the insufferable arrogance of their 'fans', the grotesque goal celebrations and the monument to shoddiness that is Highbury. Yet, the stench eminating [sic] from N5 is even more profound.... It's time to introduce you to a fellow named 'Sir' Henry Norris. Welcome to the 'proud' history of Arsenal Football Club."

Norris, as many club owners did, and continue to do, ran Arsenal as his own, private kingdom. Given the number of enemies he made down the years, this was always likely to rebound on him one day, and in 1928 Norris was banned from football for life following allegations of illegal payments made to players and other club employees (sadly John Humble, one of Arsenal's founders, also received a ban). One year previously, towards the end of the 1927–28 season, Arsenal had also been accused of throwing games, in order to ensure that Spurs were relegated. This allegation was never proved, and Arsenal had struggled all season, eventually finishing in 19th, only 3 points ahead of Spurs. Nevertheless, the allegations were enough to further worsen the relationship between the two clubs. From a Spurs point of view things were about to become far worse, as Arsenal were about to begin a period of unprecedented success.

If Norris was the father of the modern Arsenal off the pitch, Herbert Chapman was the man to do what Norris couldn't; bring Arsenal success and fame on the pitch. In doing so Chapman also came to

Arsenal Football Club Season 1920-21.

ARSENAL FOOTBALL CLUB 1920–21

Back row (l–r) Ratcliffe, Ewan, Buckley, Counley, Jim Peters, Bill Smith, Lewis, Peart, Kempton, Dunn, Wood, North, Plumb, Walden, Sir Henry Norris, Jack Humble, C. Crisp, G. Peachey, Jewett, Butler, Paterson, Leslie Knighton.

Second row (l–r) Graham, Baker, Williamson, Bradshaw, Rutherford, Joe Shaw, Hutchins, Pagnam, McKinnon.

Front row (l–r) Voysey, Rosebotham, Rose, Groves, Greenaway, Burgess, Toner, Tom Whittaker, Coupland.

equal Norris's influence off of it. It was Chapman who, in 1932, was able to persuade London Transport to rename Gillespie Road station after the club. To this day, no other football club in Britain has a train station named after them, and the value of this name change, in free advertising and prestige, is incalculable. Chapman is often referred to as being the first professional manager in British football, but he was also way ahead of his time in grasping the importance of managing the club's image, and building its brand.

Norris brought Chapman to Arsenal in 1925, an act that was to be his last significant contribution to the Arsenal story. Chapman came to Arsenal with a record of success – in fact, with Chapman as manager Huddersfield Town had enjoyed a level of success Arsenal hadn't have even come close to matching. Chapman won the League Championship in his last two seasons at Huddersfield, so it is tempting to ask why he moved at all. The likelihood is that, as well as wanting a new challenge, Chapman simply recognised Arsenal's greater potential. By this time Huddersfield's industry was already in decline, a fact which would inevitably have a knock-on effect on the town's football club. Arsenal by contrast may not have ever won much, but they were ambitious, and located in one of the largest and wealthiest cities in the world. In February 1926, less than a year after joining Arsenal, Chapman is quoted as having said the following to Tom Whittaker, who was to become a great Arsenal manager in his own right:

"I am going to make this the greatest club ground in the world, and I am going to make you the greatest trainer in the game. What do you say to that?"

(p. 70, *The Official History*)

Chapman's ambition was clear. Right from the start he wanted Arsenal to become the most famous, most prestigious club in the world.

Chapman and Norris, however, were not to see eye to eye on how

Herbert Chapman

to achieve this. Norris, despite being willing to spend a fortune on the ground, was less willing to spend large sums of money on the team itself. This predicament may well sound familiar to Arsenal's current supporters. Chapman by contrast saw spending money as the only way to guarantee success. Despite his many innovations (the use of physiotherapists, team meetings, the 'W' formation), Chapman's recipe for success was simple. Put the best players you can possibly afford on the pitch.

Arsenal tube

It was Chapman then who, very much against the wishes of Norris, turned Arsenal into the Bank of England club, able to buy any player they wished. Chapman changed Arsenal's image to such an extent, that by the time of the infamous cup defeat at the hands of Wallsall in 1933, Arsenal were widely seen as the game's aristocrats, rich, cocky and ripe for a giant-killing. It will surprise no-one that Arsenal's defeat in that game was greeted with delight around England. Arsenal at this time were some way off being loved, or even liked by neutral supporters.

Chapman's first signing for Arsenal was Charlie Buchan – significant not only because Buchan was England captain and a great player, but because it was also this deal which would eventually lead to Henry Norris's ban from football. Norris still insisted on dealing with the financial aspects of transfers himself, and though Buchan always denied it, Norris was eventually found guilty of making illegal payments to Buchan as part of the deal. For Chapman, this may have come as a blessing in disguise. Norris would never have allowed Chapman the kind of overall control he wanted, and doubtless wouldn't have let him spend the money he did either. Norris's successor as chairman was Samuel Hill-Wood, thus beginning the unbroken Hill-Wood dynasty at Arsenal. The Hill-Woods have never been interested in interfering with the football side of the club. As Jon Spurling wrote in his alternative history of Arsenal *Rebels for the Cause*:

"The Hill-Wood family's motto, which rang true until grandson Peter oversaw the Graham affair in 1995, was: Why interfere when you've got experts to do the job?"

Arsenal never won anything while Norris was still at the club, though they came close in 1927, losing the FA Cup Final to Cardiff. Norris may have laid the foundations of Arsenal's success, but he was not to be around to enjoy the benefits.

Sadly, Herbert Chapman was not to have long to enjoy his success either. On January 10th 1934 Chapman unexpectedly died, after a heavy cold turned into pneumonia. During his eight years as Arsenal manager Chapman won the league twice, and the FA Cup once, a surprisingly modest haul, given Chapman's legendary status at Arsenal, and within football as a whole. Of course, Chapman's legacy was far greater than just these three trophies, and the side he built continued to dominate the 1930s, even after his death. George Allison, who had previously been Arsenal's Managing Director took on the role of Manager, despite having no professional experience of the role. In the event this mattered little, as Joe Shaw and Tom Whittaker (who would himself eventually manage Arsenal), did most of the day to day coaching of the team. Despite criticism of Allison's appointment, and the fact that he had in effect appointed himself Manager, the set-up was a success, as Arsenal won further league titles in 1934, 1935 and 1938, as well as the FA Cup in 1936. By the end of the thirties Arsenal were one of the most famous and respected club sides in the world. Arsenal's dominance of the English game in this period is further reflected by the line up of the England team selected to play Italy in November 1934. A total of seven of the England side that day played for Arsenal.

Just as it had 25 years previously war again was to cause the suspension of professional football in England. Whereas Sir Henry Norris had previously used the suspension of the league programme during the First World War to Arsenal's advantage, the Second World War dealt Arsenal a number of near-crippling blows. Indeed, despite continuing success it is arguable that Arsenal have never quite recovered the status and dominance they enjoyed before the outbreak of war. The thirties are still referred to as Arsenal's Golden Age, and it was still Herbert Chapman's bust that greeted visitors to Highbury, right up to the point of moving out in 2006. But, given the impact Arsène Wenger has had on Arsenal, it is more than possible that in years to come his bust will join Chapman's in residence at the Emirates Stadium.

The war impacted on Arsenal both on and off the pitch. A total of 42 of Arsenal's professional playing staff joined the services during the war, and 9 of these 42 unfortunately lost their lives in the conflict. In addition, several Arsenal players, including the great Ted Drake, lost the final years of their football career to the war, age and injuries preventing them from playing on after 1945. Arsenal continued to play football during the war, competing in and winning wartime competitions such as the London League, the League South and the League South Cup. With most of the Arsenal squad active in the war effort, the team had to be bolstered with 'guest' players – basically any footballers who happened to be still in London and available to play at the time. Unsurprisingly, the honours won during these wartime competitions do not appear on Arsenal's, or any other club's, role of honour.

Highbury itself also contributed to the war effort, being used as a storage depot by ARP (Air Raid Precautions). During this time even the bitter rivalry between Arsenal and Spurs had to be put aside, and Arsenal shared White Hart Lane as their home ground from the start of the war through until September 1946. Arsenal had to share with Spurs this long after the end of the war due to the damage inflicted on Highbury by German bombers. The ground was bombed on a number of occasions, one attack resulting in the near total destruction of the North Bank, necessitating complete rebuilding after the war.

All of these factors, together with the already heavy debts incurred during the pre-war years (mainly from the building of the East and West stands in the mid-thirties), meant that Arsenal could no longer afford the best. The strain of striving to maintain Arsenal's position at, or at least near, the top finally became too much for George Allison in 1947, after 13 years as Arsenal manager. Allison handed over to Tom Whittaker, Arsenal's trainer since the days of Herbert Chapman, and immensely respected by the players.

Whittaker inherited an ageing, though still talented team, and his first season in charge proved a great success. Criticised in the papers for an allegedly defensive approach, Arsenal didn't care, for they won the 1947–48 League title. Further success followed for Whittaker, as he delivered the FA Cup in 1950, and the League again in 1953. In addition, in 1952 Arsenal were only three games away from becoming the first club to win the double in the twentieth century. With three games left to play (two in the league, and the FA cup final) Arsenal needed to win all three to secure the double.

Ted Drake

Badly affected by injuries to key players, Arsenal lost all three games, and finished the season with nothing.

Tragically Tom Whittaker was to follow in Herbert Chapman's footsteps in more ways than one. Like Chapman, Whittaker died prematurely, while still Arsenal manager, and seemingly having

Tom Whittaker

literally worked himself to death for the cause. Though not a visionary figure in the Chapman mould, Whittaker was an outstanding manager in his own right, and was utterly devoted to making Arsenal a success. Whittaker, like many Arsenal players and managers before and since, was frequently described as being an Arsenal man through and through. What exactly this means is rarely elaborated on, though maybe Joe Mercer's description of Whittaker is useful, not least because with little modification it could be equally applied to another Arsenal legend, the current manager, Arsène Wenger:

> "It is a game full of hard knocks. But Tom never hit anybody. He never shirked making a hard decision, like sacking or dropping a player, or any of the other things that can hurt deeply. But the way Tom did it, it never did. Tom made bad sportsmen into good sportsmen. He made good footballers into great footballers.... He realised the days of big buying were over. His plans only included youngsters. And every youngster who ever went to Highbury quickly learned one thing. The only thing that mattered was the club."
>
> (p. 117, *The Official History*)

Arsenal's core values are like those of any large organisation, aspirational, and not always fully lived up to. This though is what people have in mind when they talk of "a true Arsenal man", someone who believes in doing things the right way, with integrity, who values the team over the individual, who prizes hard work and effort. Somewhat old-fashioned values, and certainly the ones prized by Arsenal's old-Etonian chairman Peter Hill-Wood. At the same time, Arsenal have always been an innovative club, and one possessed of an uncompromising win at all costs mentality. These certainly seem to be the values passed down internally through the club, as former player Paul Davis describes:

> "I played for the Arsenal youth, reserve and first team. Right from day one, as a schoolboy,

you're told, 'Arsenal is different.' This club is geared to win things – finishing second is not on the agenda. Playing for Arsenal is about fighting for each other, team spirit and an 'all for one' mentality."

(p. 254, Rebels for the Cause)

That these values have sometimes conflicted with those regarding fair play and sportsmanship is undeniable, though Arsenal are hardly alone in this. Ultimately, what really matters in football, for players and fans, is to win.

After Tom Whittaker, there was to be little winning at Highbury for some time. The club subsided into a period of mediocrity, overseen first by George Swindin, and then, in a break with tradition, an outsider, the famous Billy Wright. At the time Wright was the most-capped player in the world, an England legend, but his management career was to prove undistinguished, and Arsenal came nowhere near success under him. In 1966 he was sacked after four years as manager, and the club returned to tradition in making its next appointment. Looking inside the club, Denis Hill-Wood (father of present chairman, Peter) appointed Bertie Mee, who had been Arsenal's physiotherapist since 1960. Like Allison and Whittaker before him, Mee had no previous experience as manager of a professional football club, but also like these two famous predecessors, he knew Arsenal inside out, had the respect of the players, and was unafraid of the challenge. Mee built a winning team founded on typically Arsenal values; hard work, discipline, and a trust in young players schooled in the Arsenal. Arsenal's first success under Mee was to be the European Fairs Cup (precursor to the UEFA Cup) in 1970. This was followed the next year by, finally, the double of League title and FA Cup. A fantastic achievement by an unfancied club (Arsenal had finished 12th the previous season), though gallingly Spurs had already become the first club to do the double in the twentieth century exactly 10 years previously.

Arsenal's will to win and drive were embodied at this time by the captain Frank McLintock. Arsenal's periods of success generally seem to coincide with the rise of a great, inspirational captain, someone who represents the values of the manager on the pitch. As Don Howe, Arsenal's coach at the time, and another true Arsenal man said:

"They talk about Dave Mackay and Bobby Moore as great captains, but for my money McLintock is more inspiring than either of them. I am beginning to feel obsolete in the dressing room. Frank is doing as much talking as I am – and working wonders with his words. He lifts players up and makes them feel inches taller and he continues to inspire them out there on the pitch."

(p. 138, *The Official History*)

Unlike Chapman's successes in the early thirties, this triumph didn't lead to a period of sustained success. Partly this can be attributed to the loss of Don Howe, who left after the double season to become a manager in his own right with West Bromwich Albion. Howe was to return later, again as coach, in 1977, as well as enjoying a brief spell as manager in the mid-1980s. Mee himself appeared to have run out of ideas, and was described as growing increasingly distant from the players. After sinking low enough to flirt with relegation in both 1975 and 1976, Mee announced his retirement.

The club's solution was to appoint an Arsenal man again. Terry Neill had played for the club for eleven years, and at 32 was Arsenal's youngest ever manager. His reputation, in the eyes of the fans at least, was tarnished by having previously managed Spurs. Neill was not to prove the most popular of managers in his eight years in charge. Neill never had the full respect of his players, many of whom seemed to be more interested in London's nightlife than winning things on the pitch. Neill's reign was also to bring only one trophy, the 1979 FA Cup. You could take it as a sign of bad luck, or that Neill simply wasn't a winner, that Arsenal also lost in the finals of the 1978 and 1980 FA Cups, and the 1980 UEFA Cup.

Neill was finally sacked in 1984, by which time it was apparent that the club were going nowhere under him. The weeks preceding his sacking were marked by demonstrations demanding his dismissal outside the ground, something which has not happened before or since. For better or worse (and with a couple of notable exceptions) Arsenal give their managers time in which to work, and the supporters have always been happy that this is the case. The early 1980s mediocrity was just too much to be borne indefinitely though, meaning it was only a matter of time before Neill had to go. His replacement was Don Howe, who finally got to live out his dream of managing Arsenal. Howe did a solid if unspectacular job, resigning after less than two years in charge, having got wind that Arsenal had gone behind his back and approached Terry Venables to take over his job. Howe's devotion to the club deserved better (he was later to return to the club again in a coaching capacity), and this was a prime example of Arsenal's behaviour not quite living up to its stated values.

Venables never did come to Arsenal, preferring to stay at Barcelona. Interestingly, this was the second time Arsenal missed out on Venables, as he also opted to stay with his current club (Crystal Palace) before Arsenal appointed Terry Neill. On this second occasion Arsenal again went for a former player, George Graham. George Graham was a member of the double-winning side, and had built, in a short time, a successful Millwall side based on hard work, discipline and young players. This recipe no doubt sounded familiar, and welcome to the Arsenal board, and Graham was duly installed.

It took only a year for Graham to deliver his first trophy, the 1987 League Cup. Arsenal lost in the final of the same trophy the following year, an event that will always live on in Arsenal supporters' memories as the occasion on which the hapless defender Gus Caesar trod on the ball in the penalty area, and handed victory to underdogs Luton. Real success was to follow in 1989 and 1991 when Arsenal won their first League titles since 1971. Graham built his title-winning sides on, and this will surprise no-one, hard work, discipline and young players.

The 1989 season provided possibly the most thrilling climax to a league season ever. Arsenal travelled to Anfield on 26th May 1989, needing to beat Liverpool by two clear goals to win the League. Few people gave them any chance, but they did it, the second, decisive goal being scored in the last minute by one of the youngsters, midfielder Michael Thomas. Despite this incredible finale, Graham's Arsenal sides were never much loved by the neutral. Often criticised as defensive and dirty, it is true to say that Graham's sides were more concerned with winning than playing attractive football. Nonetheless, for at least the first five years or so of Graham's reign, visitors to Highbury would have seen plenty of goals, and some very skilful young players. The likes of David Rocastle, Paul Merson, and of course Tony Adams are still venerated by fans, and were as good as any other young players produced by English clubs during this time. Unfortunately, whether down to injuries (Rocastle) or lifestyle (Merson and Adams), it is arguable whether any of these players truly fulfilled their potential. Adams deserves enormous credit for eventually getting to grips with his alcoholism, turning his life around, and captaining a second great Arsenal side, built by Arsène Wenger. It is significant too, that, once freed from the constrictions of playing under the utilitarian Graham, Adams finally turned into the player those who saw him as a youngster always thought he could be: a skilful, ball-playing centre-back, not just a mere stopper, albeit an exceptional one.

When Graham was sacked in 1995, there was little doubt that the side had stagnated. Like Neill's Arsenal, this Arsenal side were capable of winning cups (the FA Cup and League Cup in 1993, and the Cup Winner's Cup in 1994) but were nowhere in the League.

Though this no doubt influenced the board's thinking, it wasn't this that led to Graham's sacking. Rather, it was the allegation that following the transfers of two players, Pal Lydersen and John Jensen, Graham had pocketed £425,000, money the club felt was rightfully theirs. The exact truth of the matter is still unclear, with Graham still protesting his innocence, but few tears were shed for Graham at the time. Whoever the money rightfully belonged to, few people thought it right that the manager of the club should benefit financially from transfer deals, particularly given Graham's insistence on high standards of behaviour and notorious tightness when it came to negotiating player contracts.

Michael Thomas scores the winner at Anfield, 1989

After a few months with Stewart Houston as caretaker manager, Bruce Rioch took over as Arsenal manager. Rioch was another tough, disciplinarian Scot, though the Bolton side he had managed previously did at least have a reputation for playing attacking football. Rioch had no previous links with the club, and seemed to have problems getting on with the players, most notably the fan's idol Ian Wright, from the start. Arsenal's Rioch did play far better football than in previous seasons, and having finally spent some big money on world-class players (Dennis Bergkamp and David Platt) Arsenal finished fifth, good enough to qualify for the UEFA Cup. At this point in Arsenal's history this qualified as success. But it wasn't enough to save Rioch. Some have suggested that Rioch was only ever intended as a stop-gap measure until Arsène Wenger became available, but it is more likely that vice-chairman David Dein, who by this point was the dominant force within the club, simply lost all confidence in Rioch to deliver. Dein has always taken more of an interest in on than off-pitch affairs at Highbury, and the complaints of senior players, Wright amongst them, would have been heard out by Dein.

Arséne Wenger was a friend of David Dein's, but was pretty much unknown to anyone else at Highbury, or English football for that matter. In 1996, despite the influx of foreign players caused by the advent of the cash-rich Premiership in 1992, there was still little interest in football outside England. Thus, the fact that Wenger had guided Monaco to the French title, and the semi-finals of the Champions League meant little to anyone in England. That he was currently employed by Grampus Eight, a Japanese team, meant even less. But, it didn't take long to win over the doubters. A key moment for most Arsenal fans was the debut of Patrick Vieira. Vieira actually made his debut before Wenger officially assumed control of the club. However, everyone knew that Wenger was responsible for his signing, and so the credit went to him when Vieira came off the bench to inspire a previously lacklustre Arsenal side to a 4–1 win over Sheffield Wednesday.

Despite being linked with Real Madrid (and others) almost every summer, Patrick Vieira stayed at Arsenal for nine years. Arsène Wenger's first signing went on to become his captain, until his eventual departure for Juventus in 2005. As previously mentioned, every great Arsenal side has had a great captain. Not that Vieira's performances were always consistently great. When they were though, Arsenal were twice the team they were without him. Much

Arsène Wenger with the Premership trophy

like Wenger, Vieira is not a shouter and a bawler, and prefers to lead by example. In this respect, the whole team did rely on their captain's individual form far more than they did when Tony Adams or Frank McLintock were captain. Those players were great leaders irrespective of their individual performances, where Vieira was a much quieter character. Upon Vieira's departure Wenger was quick to appoint Thierry Henry as captain. It will be interesting to observe how Thierry Henry – in terms of skill a far greater player than any of his predecessors as captain – goes about his new role of leading the Arsenal.

Wenger has now won three Premiership titles and four FA Cups in his first eight years at Highbury. Only the Champions League remains out of reach. Wenger's critics are quick to point out that they will never be regarded as a truly great club until they do win it. Though harsh, there is an element of truth in this. In order to join the ranks of the truly world-famous super clubs (and super brands), Arsenal do need to take this next step. To a large extent, that is the motivation behind the stadium move – to give Arsenal the resources to win the Champions League, and join the likes of former winners Real Madrid, AC Milan and Manchester United. To Wenger's enormous credit, he pushed for the stadium move to happen, even though he knew that it would severely curtail his transfer budget for a number of seasons, and that it would be his eventual successor who would reap the full benefits.

Wenger, like so many Arsenal men before him, put the good of the club ahead of his own personal gain.

Honours

League Champions
1930/31, 1932/33, 1933/34, 1934/35, 1937/38,
1947/48, 1952/53, 1970/71, 1988/89,
1990/91, 1997/98, 2001/02, 2003/04

FA Cup
1930,1936, 1950, 1971,1979,
1993, 1998, 2002, 2003, 2005

League Cup
1987, 1993

European Fairs Cup
(Now UEFA Cup)
1970

European Cup Winner's Cup
1994

We are Arsenal

"There was a way of being at Arsenal. The saying was 'Remember who you are, remember what you are, and remember who you play for'. That's what they used to say to us."

Don Howe

Perhaps all that's changed with branding in the last fifty years is that we've become better at analysing it. Until relatively recent times things were done by instinct and never given a 'brand' label. So when Herbert Chapman persuaded London Underground to rename Gillespie Road station 'Arsenal' in 1932, his instincts were those of a particularly shrewd modern brand manager. But of course he realised the absolute importance of that first principle of branding: Get the product right. It was Chapman's successes on the pitch, unprecedented at the time, that created the Arsenal legend that in turn made Arsenal a brand recognised around the world.

So for a football brand like Arsenal nothing matters so much as the players themselves. Yet there is something of a paradox here because football is above all a team game. A united team will beat 11 brilliant but disconnected individuals. So Arsenal, perhaps more than any other football club, has always stressed: no player, is bigger than the club. In modern terms no player is bigger than the brand either and the association with the brand will be ended if a player fails to live up to its values. There are examples from Jimmy Logie (sacked in the 1950s for 'unsporting behaviour') to George Graham (removed as manager in the 1990s for personally profiting from transfer deals) to Jermaine Pennant (jailed in 2005 for drunk driving on top of many other episodes of indiscipline). If judged only on performance, each of these would have stayed but Arsenal insist that they demand more than just footballing ability. They require players to accept the ethos that success comes from shared commitment and dedication. The misdemeanours of Tony Adams, the captain who confessed to being an alcoholic and was jailed for drunk driving, were worse than, say, Jermaine Pennant. But mature remorse and a renewed commitment to his team mates and fans meant that Tony's position was never under threat. He could still hold his head high and say "I am Arsenal".

Of course, this means that away from the cases above that made headlines, there have been thousands of cases of players moved on because they failed to adapt to the ethos. A theme runs through the remarks of former players about their time at the Arsenal: it took dedication, inner belief and a lot of effort. For the fans, watching on, individual failures can often be tinged with regret. Players like Peter Marinello, Alan Hudson, Vladimir Petrovic, Charlie Nicholas and Nicholas Anelka come along every ten years or so, stars that burn brightly for a brief period then fizzle out. For their time they are the fans' favourite, then a realisation dawns that, brilliant as they are, they are not pulling their weight for the team. The fans, brand loyalists, recognise that they are undermining the values they hold dear and by which they live.

Each player, therefore, has to adapt to the brand ethos that is deeply imbedded in Arsenal's history. There is an Arsenal way, everyone acknowledges it, but no one knows how to define it with any precision. But this is the situation with most brands, even those that have made the greatest efforts to define themselves. There is an IBM way, for example, but the 'men in blue suits' stereotype is rejected for its simplistic inaccuracy.

The way you can understand brands most tangibly is through their people. Football is a prime example of that. In this chapter we will explore what the Arsenal brand is really about through four outstanding representatives in the modern period. The individuals we have chosen are all Arsenal captains. A football captain is not chosen for strategic skills, as in cricket, but because he represents what the manager and the club are trying to instil in their team. Symbolically, therefore, the captaincy is a vital position. The captain really is the brand representative. The players on the pitch need to look up to him and regard him as their leader. The manager relies on him as his man on the pitch. And the fans need to admire him as a role model.

We chose Frank McLintock, Pat Rice, Tony Adams and Patrick Vieira. These four have captained Arsenal through most of the last 40 years. In the periods when they were not captain Arsenal won no trophies. So they are not controversial choices. Yet there is significance in the fact that none of them were footballers gifted with an amazing natural talent. Each of them succeeded as a player by force of character rather than silky football skills. You might point to others as 'brand icons' in the sense that they inspired more hero worship purely as players: Charlie George under Frank McLintock's captaincy, Liam Brady with Pat Rice, first David Rocastle then Ian Wright and Dennis Bergkamp under Tony Adams, Thierry Henry with Patrick Vieira. But, being as objective as possible, these great players represent aspects of the brand rather than its absolute essence. To understand the essence we need to know the captains.

Frank McLintock: Arsenal captain 1964–74

So we started by meeting Frank McLintock. Frank's career ran through the sixties and the first half of the seventies. Those were days when footballers were paid less than plumbers and train drivers. Football really was the working class game and its finances reflected the low wages of its supporters. In the early 1960s footballers' wages were capped; there was a maximum wage set at around the average earnings of a working man, and there was no freedom of contract. George Eastham, then at Newcastle, rebelled against this, effectively going on one-man strike. When he joined Arsenal in 1960 he made it possible for footballers to earn much higher wages.

Frank McLintock joined Arsenal in 1964 when this revolution was just getting under way. By the end of his career players were earning wages that ensured they could live comfortably but the financial gap between then and now is enormous. Frank's house, therefore, is a perfectly pleasant, affluent suburban detached in Winchmore Hill. It probably reflects the fact that his post-football career in business and the media has been steadily successful rather that that he made a fortune as a footballer. But Thierry Henry lives half a dozen miles away in a £6 million house in Hampstead.

Frank is at home in the suburban surroundings where we meet. His wife Barbara opens the door and offers tea or coffee while Frank

ARSENAL

FRANK McLINTOCK

stands in the kitchen doorway chatting to his grandchildren who have just finished school for the day. We talk in the living room, a room furnished in very traditional style. This place is solid, honest, unflashy. Frank himself is courteous and eloquent as he starts talking about his Arsenal days.

"I signed for a record British fee (£80,000). I'd been tapped up by Arsenal(!) and they'd told me they were also after Gordon Banks and Ray Wilson. I decided to leave Leicester for higher honours, even though it was going great at Leicester. There was a good structure there with Matt Gillies as manager. But I was ambitious.

You recognise quickly that Arsenal is a big club. Expectations and disappointments are higher. We'd go on a pre-season tour of Iceland and find 50/60 people waiting for the coach. You didn't get that at Leicester.

Being manager was a new job for Billy Wright. Here we had the biggest club with an inexperienced manager. I was guilty of stirring things up a bit – I thought no one knew what they were doing. After the settled structure at Leicester it was a shock.

My move wasn't about money. I was only on £55 a week. I didn't get too worked up about money because I didn't think I'd get it – we had no agents or lawyers then.

On the field I ran around like a blue-arsed fly. I showed over-keenness, determination, good faults but not helping the cause. There was a heavy burden of history. I got them to change the strip for a season – bloody cheek, eh? – to all red without white sleeves. Just to get away from the history. The club hadn't won anything for years after all that success in the thirties."

Growing up and supporting Arsenal in the 1950s was a difficult time for an Arsenal fan. As Frank says, there was all that tradition. Stories of Alex James, Cliff Bastin and Eddie Hapgood, stars of the 1930s, were told because no one had come along since to really match them.

After some League and FA Cup success in the late forties and early fifties, a long fallow period followed, with never a whiff of success. Arsenal seemed to be moribund, weighed down by its history. Even so it was still shocking to hear that it was Frank McLintock who had changed the most visible sign of Arsenal's identity – the red shirt with white sleeves – to an all-red shirt for one season. This had always been seen as a Billy Wright initiative, and Wright himself had been seen by most fans as an outsider who did not understand Arsenal's traditions.

"An awful lot needed to be done. Changing the shirt didn't really work. But there were three important things that happened. First Bertie Mee took over, which was a massive surprise. Bertie had been the physiotherapist, not really a football playing man. But, secondly, he appointed Dave Sexton as coach and he was a lovely man. Third, there was a decent youth policy. There were good kids like George Armstrong, John Radford, Jon Sammels, Peter Simpson, Pat Rice, Eddie Kelly and David Court coming through.

Bertie Mee knew how to run an organisation, he believed in discipline, was as hard as nails. If you were injured, he wouldn't let you sit around with a cup of tea. So you'd hate being injured.

He had the intelligence to let Dave Sexton get on with it. Things improved. Then Sexton left – and another major surprise, Don Howe was made coach. He was a player, one of us. But after a week he really laid into us, and he was an outstanding coach. (Can't understand why Arsène got rid of him, he'd sort out the defence.)

So there was a steady graph of improvement. Credit Bertie Mee, Dave Sexton, Don Howe. I've played in seven cup finals – it's destroying to get beat in the final. Lost to Swindon and Leeds in finals (Jack Charlton fouled the goalie, it was outrageous).

I was an influential player without realising it. We played in

Europe, the Fairs Cup. The difference in style was interesting. Continental teams probe. In the final we went to Anderlecht and I thought this is going to be OK. Probe, probe. Found ourselves 3–0 down and we hadn't broken sweat. Ray Kennedy came on, scored and I saw they couldn't head the ball. So we used that in the second leg – I told the team 'We can do it'.

We won the second leg 3-0 and the cup. We played like a team of demons, tore into them. Their players asked "Are you on drugs?" But we were an athletic team, we had to be, played at a high tempo, closed down collectively. And we had the shortest defence in the League."

As our interview progressed Frank became more and more animated. Now he was on his feet, showing me how to mark a man, how to defend corners, how to use your arms and body weight. Above all, how to use your intelligence on a football pitch. The more he moved the more he seemed to grow in stature. You could see that this man was a real leader on the pitch and you could sense that there was still a passion burning inside him for football – and for the Arsenal. Pat Rice would later talk about Frank's 'inner drive' – here it was, almost tangible, an energy radiating from a man now in his mid-60s. At a time when the Arsenal defence had been heavily criticised for conceding too many goals from set pieces, it seemed a shame that this defensive masterclass was not given to the 2005 team. Yet when Frank joined Arsenal, he had arrived as midfielder, not a defender. He was moved to centre-back after a couple of years.

"No, I didn't want to switch to centre-back. They thought I'd burn myself out in midfield. I did lots of silly running. At the back you run less but mentally you have to be on the ball.

Geoff Hurst said West Ham practised for a week before playing us and still they couldn't find a way through. We could lose the current team on tactics. We were mean not dirty, marked slightly in front of the forwards, always together as a unit.

Arsène I like and he's done a fantastic job. He's single-minded, as great managers are, so he's a bit stubborn. I talk to him about some basics they're not doing and he says 'Well, they should know'. There's no Plan B, no Niall Quinn to bring on. A lack of physical meanness. An abundance of skill but not enough strength.

Charlie George came in. Just a boy who hadn't filled out properly. Especially in training he did wonderful things. We'd look at each and think 'How?' He came on a bundle, had a great shot, was a cocky bastard. But he got nervous before games, he was physically sick before he went out. But there was a touch of arrogance there, you need that. And he still watches Arsenal. When he scored at Wembley to win the double, he laid flat on his back – we'd never seen anything like that. It was the first unusual goal celebration.

Next season we were seventh and I got the players together, sent away the coaches, and I just laid into them. "I want to know why" – we need to improve. As captain I used to lay into George Graham (my best mate), you have to get your point across. It was a knowledgeable, tactical team – we worked at it.

When I left I had a big bust-up with Bertie Mee. He dropped me for the first time. Bob McNab went to him, said 'Frank's your driving force, you can't do that'. Bertie wouldn't have it. So they sold me, I was 34, for £35,000. A big fee so no chance for a bit of money for me. And just short of a 10-year testimonial.

Arsenal's an upstairs/downstairs kind of place. I was the only one ever to go into the offices at Arsenal. It's still like that – like 'royalty'. David Dein's closer to the players. You're greeted well when you're there, but you're never invited. I've bought a box in the new stadium with two or three colleagues."

Frank's back on his feet again, it's time for another little coaching session. Given half a chance Frank would still be out there, kicking a ball around. He talks affectionately about his old team mates, particularly the Double team of 1970–71. Bob McNab still rings him from America, he sees George Graham, Sammy Nelson, Jon Sammels and Pat Rice sometimes. Peter Simpson lives up the road. He's in regular contact with Bob Wilson, Charlie George, Eddie Kelly, Peter Marinello and John Radford.

"Arsenal's a special club – it binds you together. The dressing rooms, marble halls, heated floors. You could have done an operation in the dressing room, it was that clean. Arsenal will always have good people – doctors, behind the scenes people. We had X-ray machines 41 years ago. When we were abroad we flew in two planes, always wore collar and tie, like the Army.

Highbury is wonderful but you have to move on. Life goes on. The modern players won't have the same reverence. The training ground's more important to them now in a way. But the Emirates stadium will make a difference. It means we'll be catching up, not a million away as we are at the moment – Real Madrid, Barcelona, Juventus, Milan."

It's striking that we've talked – inevitably – about the past but Frank has no nostalgic desire to dwell there. He's already excited by what is to come. The same fire that had him changing the strip to lose the ghosts of the past is still burning. It's the future that matters.

Pat Rice: Arsenal captain 1976–80

It's not easy finding the Arsenal training ground. There are no signs outside to announce it. If you were walking by you would see a small notice saying 'Players will not sign autographs' and that would give you a clue. Otherwise you drive past it, on a country road, unaware that 100 metres down a little lane are the country's best training facilities for footballers. The players and staff know their way there: that's all that matters.

ARSENAL

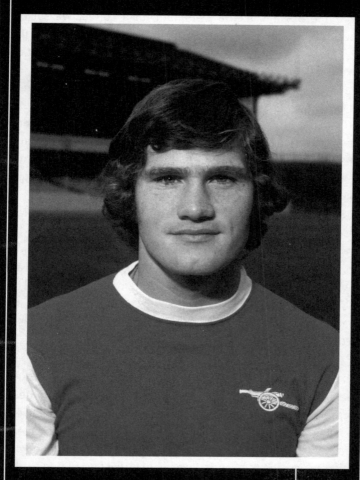

PAT RICE

Slightly flustered by being late I jumped out of my car and headed for Reception. Sol Campbell happened to be coming out as I was going in. Pat Rice, who had been chatting to receptionists, was waiting for me inside the door. Instead of fining me for lateness he took me upstairs to the restaurant for a coffee. We sat on a settee while, in the background, Arsène Wenger continued a post-lunch chat with coach Boro Primorac. It was a week of international matches so few players were around.

Pat started enthusing about the training ground. "When the Boss came he wanted his own – we used to rent from UCL but we didn't have it all the times we wanted. Then the changing rooms burnt down so we had to use Sopwell House. It was lucky the farmer wanted to sell all this land, just at the right time. Arsène had a big influence on every detail. Everything was designed with the needs of the players in mind."

I took him back to his beginnings.

"I was born in Belfast then came over at the age of nine. My mother wanted to keep the family together, and my brother was in Manchester (a plumber). We all settled in Islington. I lived in Pools Park then Avenell Road then Monsell Road then Gillespie Road. Went to St Joan of Arc school in Blackstock Road then William of York Secondary.

I supposed he'd been spotted by Arsenal playing for his school team or Islington. "Oh no, there was a guy called Mickey Doolan, connected to Tottenham, who picked the two best players from each school team. I was one which meant I played for Islington District against Tottenham. I was told by Bill Bailey, who ran schools football for the FA, that I 'wasn't good enough' – and he was right. Anyway, I was very lucky, I was told I could come along and train at Arsenal.

I came nowhere near the ability level. I made up for it through endeavour. Made myself fitter and stronger.

Coming from Ireland, I was a Man United fan but I was at

the pre-Munich match that Arsenal lost 5–4. I changed my allegiance then.

Arsenal said I could come and train the following year. There were 45–60 players. The day I signed as an apprentice, Micky Boot became a professional. At that point I'd left school and was working at a greengrocers and the manager was good to me, promised me my own shop by the age of 21. Arsenal seemed a big risk but I took it.

I made my debut at 19. Whenever we played Everton, Alan Ball was the problem. So Peter Storey was moved to midfield to mark him and I came in at right back.

Frank McLintock was a massive figure. We all knew about his cup experience, always losing in finals. He had this inner drive to succeed. But they were all personalities in that Double team. Bob McNab, Raddy, George Graham, Geordie Armstrong. Once, playing Wolves, I made out I was Jack the Lad and did a trick that went wrong. The whole lot of them, led by Frank, came over and gave me a bollocking you won't forget. I never did that again.

There was the history all round – photos of Chapman, the 1930s teams. We wanted to make our own name, we were young plus we had the experience of Frank. There was drive from Don Howe and Bertie Mee (amazing organiser, nothing left to chance). Don had this never-say-die Midlands spirit.

That was our background, we were working class. We knew we had to strive and work, not knowing the meaning of defeat.

Years later I was the survivor of the team and Terry Neill (we'd had moments of disagreement) amazed me by making me Captain. You have to talk to play in the Back Four, you rely on that, and it's no hardship to me to talk and make a decision. If you make the wrong decision, you learn, don't do it again. Tony Adams had that too, without a doubt.

There were successes. We won the FA Cup against Manchester United, but the team was changing. Liam Brady went to Italy. He was young, but I was at the end of my career. I went to play for

12th May 1979 ARSENAL SKIPPER PAT RICE HOLDS ALOFT THE FA CUP TROPHY AT WEMBLEY AFTER HIS TEAM BEAT MANCHESTER UNITED 3–2 IN THE FINAL.

Watford. John Devine had been groomed to take my place at right back and he did well. When I left, the pressure was off him and John Hollins (who was older than me) switched to right back. But I had to join Watford to continue playing. I'd been offered the player/manager job at Millwall, but Bertie Mee got on the phone and said 'don't do anything till you talk to Graham Taylor' [the Watford manager].

I thought that was it when I left Arsenal. I always try to look forward, not back. Arsenal owed me nothing, they gave me a chance, I was the luckiest man alive to get it.

At Watford I became Graham Taylor's 'manager on the pitch'. Then I started training their schoolboys Monday to Friday. At a pre-season training meeting Graham Taylor said 'There's Don Howe on the phone, he wants to talk to you.' Don, Arsenal's manager then, asked me back to run the Youth team.

I wasn't sure. I thought if not then, it'll be never. You don't get a second chance to go back. Watford were going to pay me more to stay, with a longer contract but no guarantee of my own team. That's what clinched it. I wanted a team.

For twelve years I ran Arsenal's youth teams. Then Bruce Rioch came in as manager and moved me up, alongside Stewart Houston. It didn't work out for Bruce, Arsène arrived and asked me to be his Assistant. I was more than willing to accept.

Arsène brought a calmness to everyone. It takes a lot for him to raise his voice. When things go bad he stays calm but it's cutting him up inside. You see in his face that he doesn't like to lose. Other managers are different (George would be blistering one to one, Don gave you hell, Bruce was the biggest ranter of the lot). What they have in common is they're all passionate to win. You can't knock George for his football, he won the trophies.

Now we have all these young players. Fabregas... Eboue (so quick just needs to learn positional sense then he's got everything), Flamini, Clichy. And watch for Matthew Connolly, only 16. [There was a brief exchange later in the gym between Pat and Steve Bould as Connolly had trained with the First Team today – 'He was great. Just needs to work on his stamina.'] You pick a team to win a game. Nationality doesn't matter. The price of English players is double. If you haven't got technique and pace today you haven't got a chance."

I suggested he might have struggled to make it today.

"I hope my story could be repeated. I got lucky. I was given loads of help by Arsenal. You need honesty. I say to young players 'I'll tell you no lies. When you don't play well, I'll give you a bollocking. When you do play well, I'll praise you to the skies'.

If you're going to fail, make sure you fail for lack of ability, not for lack of effort.

The new stadium is about competing. We need to move on. We see other teams of lower status spending more, but I'm not envious of them. Look at our Academy. But beware – when you've got a 60,000 stadium you need to have a team to fill it. Arsenal knows that. It's why we've invested in youth."

As we finished, I got up and thanked him and he said "Do you want a look around?" "Only if you've got time," I said. " It'll only take ten minutes." It took thirty.

Just off the restaurant was the team meeting room. It used to be the press room but Arsène hated the press mixing with the players – so now there are press facilities in a building 50 yards away.

Downstairs at reception we put on plastic overshoes (like surgeons wear) – red, of course. Then Pat took us through into the changing rooms – big, spacious, light. (Arsène specified lots of natural light.) There's a boot room off it where all the boots are on numbered pegs. The apprentices no longer clean the boots (not allowed by law apparently). Pat thinks it mollycoddles the kids who don't get the value of work. There are white tiles everywhere, steam room, showers, massage room, everything clinically clean. The treatment room where I was introduced to physiotherapist Colin Lewin (Gary's son – Gary away with England). There's a hydrotherapy pool and a jacuzzi.

There is a strong sense of hierarchy. The youth team changing rooms are at the other end, very similar, but smaller. Just as the youngsters use the far end of the restaurant. I asked where Fabregas sits – "With the first team, it's where all the young players want to be."

Then we went outside and there are pitches everywhere. The nearest one is not used. "It's the Geordie Armstrong memorial pitch – he collapsed over there." The youth teams have their pitches, the reserves and then the first team. Steve Braddock is now groundsman here (switched from Highbury) and all the grounds are immaculate.

"The youngsters know if I've been around. If I find a pair of dirty boots I chuck them in the bushes over there."

Into the gym, where bicycles, weight machines, mats, equipment are all around. Just three people are there. Cesc Fabregas cycling away, with a physio next to him, and Steve Bould doing stretching exercises. A little banter between Pat and Cesc about Spain doing badly last night. "Boro's gonna see you," says Pat. "He already has," says Cesc. "When I saw him he did that" (punches the air above his head with both hands). Boro Primorac is Serbian, Cesc Fabregas is Spanish – Serbia had just beaten Spain 1–0 in an Under-21 international.

As with Frank McLintock there is immense pride in achievements but a natural determination to keep looking to the future. His own story and character are examples of a narrative thread that has run through the history of Arsenal. The achievement of success through effort and teamwork, rather than through individual brilliance, has led to the club being labelled 'Lucky Arsenal' in the 1930s and 'Boring Boring Arsenal' in the 1990s. This in turn leads to an attitude of defiance: "We don't care what you say, we are Arsenal."

ARSENAL

TONY ADAMS

Tony Adams: Arsenal captain 1988–2002

Finding Tony Adams became a quest and one that we failed. We wanted to meet him because it would have been good to meet him, but Tony proved elusive. We hunted him through footballing contacts, the ghost-writer of his book, a friend who'd befriended him during his poetry and piano-learning days in South London, and the Sporting Chance Clinic. Eventually a pleasant man named Stuart phoned to say that Tony was very sorry and very busy, with not five minutes to spare.

We had to respect that. Anyway, we had followed his career for twenty years and we felt we knew him. We understood too that he was now a diplomat and would not be keen to say anything controversial. So we happily opted for other sources. Interviewed by Brian Viner in the *Independent* after he had finally retired from Arsenal and was manager of Wycombe Wanderers, Tony said: "Well, it's very hard for me to comment on Arsenal. I rarely see them play because I've got my eyes elsewhere now. But that doesn't mean I don't love 'em. I was there for 19 years and that's a big part of my life."

Our interest is in the way that Tony Adams represented the qualities of the Arsenal brand. It is extraordinary how he managed to do so at various stages of his career while morphing from one personality into a completely different one. So we need to review the changes in that personality over 19 years and, in doing so, we'll understand how the Arsenal brand changed too.

Brands succeed because people feel they have a relationship with the brand that goes beyond the purely utilitarian. Football brands rely on the personalities (mainly players) who embody them. Do you relate to this brand? Do you relate to this player? Nick Hornby talks about everyone at Highbury relating to Tony Adams. Questioned "Why?" he says: "The answer is obvious, and it's got very little to do with his nationality and everything to do with his character. Or characters."

Nick Hornby was making this point in the context of weary media commentators bemoaning the lack of English players in top teams. They express a fear that fans are not able to relate to foreign imports as deeply as they do to local lads. In fact, as Nick Hornby says, there was far more of a problem relating to the typical George Graham midfield – Jimmy Carter, David Hillier, Ian Selley, Eddie McGoldrick! The brand, personified by the players, now has a cosmopolitan element. Do we relate to Thierry Henry? Yes, please, if he'll let us into his family. But back in the 1980s, Tony Adams stood for the values Arsenal fans aspired to.

Tony Adams was born in Essex in 1966, an important year for English football. He represented England Schoolboys and could have joined many top clubs including Manchester United. He chose Arsenal because he felt he would receive the best coaching there. In the same room, on the same day, five other youngsters agreed to join Arsenal: David Rocastle, Martin Hayes, Martin Keown, Michael Thomas and Gus Caesar. Terry Burton, the youth team manager, later described it as "a good day at the office".

By the age of 15, Tony was playing for the reserve team. It was already clear that he was a star in the making. "Quiet determination was my style", although Tony was soon adding a lot more volume to go with the determination. He made his first-team debut at the age of 17, one of the youngest players to represent Arsenal. Early in his career there was more than just exceptional physique to distinguish him. He was a good listener and he adopted an idea from Pat Rice who had told him he used to keep records of all the wingers he played against while winning the Double. Tony started taking notes, storing them on an early PC, about each of the opponents he faced.

This was an indication that there had always been a more cerebral person wanting to come out. But these were now the years of George Graham's managership and there was little encouragement for players who wished to analyse football. George Graham had taken over as manager from Don Howe in 1986 and he instilled a new intensity into training. As a player George had been skilful, sophisticated and lazy, earning him the nickname 'Stroller'.

As a manager he veered towards the opposite. The word 'resilience' became the word of the moment and of every season under George Graham. Tony Adams talks about running followed by more running, a hard physical training regime that led to repetitive work on set-pieces. The aim was to ensure that everyone knew their job and their responsibilities to the team. 'Keeping shape' became a mantra. But organisation, teamwork and unity developed, and they became instinctive.

In 1987 Arsenal beat Liverpool, against all expectations, in the Littlewoods Cup Final at Wembley. The Liverpool team were all-conquering at that time, at home and abroad, with Dalglish, Rush and Hansen in a team of stars. Arsenal had a team of raw youngsters, with a 20-year-old Tony Adams at the heart of the defence. Tony had been ever-present in league and cup competitions that season and he won his first England cap in a spectacular 4–2 victory over Spain in Madrid. Now he faced Liverpool at Wembley and within 15 minutes Ian Rush had scored. "When Rush scores Liverpool wins" was the oracular statement that everyone believed. Tony Adams represented the spirit of Arsenal's resistance. Arsenal stormed back in the second half and won 2–1. A fanzine title was born: 1–0 down, 2–1up.

Less than a year later, George Graham appointed Tony Adams as captain at the age of 21. He took over form the vastly more experienced Kenny Sansom, and became the youngest captain in Arsenal's history. He admitted that his interpretation of the role of the captain then was to shout a lot and tell others what to do to defend. At times Arsenal fans still get nostalgic about such simplicity. For the new captain the game was about winning. Failure to win – as happened in the 1988 Final against Luton and with England in Euro 88 – was taken hard. "I did not like the feeling of failure and it fuelled a determination to go back and succeed." He wanted to prove himself, and to prove others wrong – that was at the heart of what he did and it chimed completely with the spirit of Arsenal. Jeered at as a 'donkey' by opposition fans, he heard the chants, resented them but almost wore the badge with pride.

It implies a ruthlessness that was undoubtedly there. Tony Adams has written that a team needs only respect for each other not affection. But it is clear too that the Arsenal team of the late eighties and early nineties liked each other too. This was largely because they had grown up together, with Adams, Merson, Rocastle and Thomas all coming up through the ranks at the same time. This is almost impossible to imagine in football now – or, if it happened, the players would all have different nationalities. But then, particularly with English clubs excluded from Europe since the Heysel tragedy, football was much more parochial. It was easier to build team spirit if you gathered players from similar backgrounds and nationalities.

The general view was that drinking encouraged team spirit too. "A team that drinks together, wins together" seemed to be the accepted thought. When it came to drinking to build team spirit, Arsenal's captain led by example. He established a Tuesday drinking club that, for him, spread to most other days of the week. And the drinking seemed to be working. In 1989, with almost the last kick of the match, Arsenal won the league championship in the most dramatic finale in history. Michael Thomas scored to make the score 2–0 against Liverpool at Anfield. A lot of drinking followed that victory.

It became apparent that the drinking had got out of hand when, just before Christmas 1990, Tony Adams was convicted of drink driving and sent to prison. In his book *Addicted*, Tony made no attempt to excuse his drunkenness. Although his conviction was a shock to him and the club at the time, he is now concerned only to emphasise how wrong his behaviour was. Yet, after release from prison, after returning to the side having spent eight weeks inside, the drinking went on for another six years. So, remarkably, did the winning. In 1991, just released from prison, he led Arsenal to win the League championship convincingly. In 1993 Arsenal won the Cup double, and in 1994, against the odds, beat Parma in the final of the European Cup-Winners Cup.

Eventually the excesses started to catch up with Tony Adams and Arsenal. In 1995 George Graham was sacked as manager for taking 'bungs'. Tony's regular response to his own and other people's problems was to drink and keep drinking. As fans we all thought we knew Tony Adams. Yet none of us noticed that his performances were becoming affected by his drinking. On his own admission he would easily have failed a breathalyser test before several first team matches.

In the summer of 1996 England's defeat in the European Championships triggered a bender and another self-destructive period of drinking. After much agonising and in a spirit of desperation, Tony Adams confessed to being an alcoholic. He started attending Alcoholics Anonymous and he made his failings brutally clear to team mates and the media. The world began to see a different Tony Adams, first one abased by the humiliation of addiction to alcohol, then a hero rising from the lowest points of his life. We saw the qualities that had made him formidable despite his drinking habits. Now we understood more clearly the real strength of character that had made him a remarkable player and captain. The 'donkey' jibes stopped and he transformed himself into the most honest and brutally self-critical of modern footballers. No longer the 'Charlie Big Potatoes' that he ridiculed himself for having been, he now came to define the model of a team player.

This transformation of Adams the brand coincided with the transformation of Arsenal the brand by Arsène Wenger. The 'studious Frenchman' arrived in the autumn of 1996, replacing Bruce Rioch as manager. There was suspicion at first on the part of Tony Adams. Like other footballers he withholds immediate respect from those who have not 'done it'. Arsène Wenger had no great playing record to admire. He arrived at Arsenal from Japan and relative obscurity.

We can imagine a certain amount of mutual sizing-up. No doubt each was suspicious of the other. But soon they realised that they were both moving in the same direction, and there never seemed to be a serious doubt that captain Adams was the manager's representative on the pitch. This role would have been impossible for an unreformed alcoholic working under Arsène Wenger. When Wenger arrived, any lasting vestiges of a drinking culture had to disappear, driven out by a fanatical attention to diet, fitness and conditioning. And there is now no doubt that, for a recovering alcoholic going from day to day in a personal battle against drink, this was a welcome shift in culture. Tony Adams no longer had to isolate himself by refusing to drink. Sobriety became the norm.

The repercussions for football were enormous. Tony Adams' confessions, alongside those of team mate Paul Merson (addicted to alcohol and gambling), led to a new professionalism in English football at the senior level. For Arsenal, guided by Adams and Wenger, they ushered in a period of unprecedented success. Although he had been successful under George Graham – two championships, an FA Cup and two League Cups – Arsenal now moved up to a higher level within the Premiership that had first come into being in 1994.

So, in 1998, just two years after the arrival of Arsène Wenger and two years after the rehabilitation of Tony Adams, Arsenal won the League and FA Cup double – for the first time since the team captained by Frank McLintock in 1971.

These were the golden years of Tony Adams' career, the years under Arsène Wenger. Although the major football relationship of his career was with George Graham ('desire plus talent equals success'), Arsène Wenger enabled Tony to break free from the 'Son of George' caricature. Fear was no longer a factor in motivating players. There was an obsession with standards every bit as steely-eyed, but it was surrounded by a greater awareness of a wider world. This fitted well with the personal hinterland that Tony was now exploring, the arts, education, relationships.

Tony Adams went away from Arsenal on a high note. In his last season Arsenal again won the Double. His performances were outstanding. The maturity he had gained off the field showed on the field. Tony Adams sprayed the ball around from the back like Bobby Moore or Beckenbauer in the year of his birth. This final period had been signalled when Arsenal won the Double in 1998. In the final match of the season at Highbury, Arsenal clinched the title by beating Everton 4–0. The final goal, in the final minutes, was scored by the man who had been captain for more than a decade. Breaking forward from the back, running onto a chipped pass from Steve Bould, Tony Adams took the ball just inside the Everton penalty area. With his left foot he struck the ball on the half-volley into the corner of the Everton net. Nothing could have expressed the transformation of Tony Adams more convincingly or more fittingly. He had taken a journey in his life, and we had followed it through his football. At that moment 38,000 fans in Highbury were united in pride for the man and the club.

Patrick Vieira: Arsenal captain 2002–2005

Arsenal Football Club protects its modern-day players as if they were gold bullion inside Fort Knox – which in a sense they are. They are valuable properties. They are further protected by personal layers of security such as lawyers and agents whose purpose is to cocoon the footballer client until agreed sums of money have exchanged hands. The modern footballer is a brand, sometimes loosely attached to the values of the football club brand. A book such as this would not have been written ten years ago, but there is now no point standing like King Canute against the tide of commercialism. To do so would be to deny yourself the pleasure of watching the likes of Thierry Henry and Patrick Vieira.

But a brand is not just about commercial value. Seeing brands only in terms of financial worth is a blinkered approach. Brands are much more interesting, certainly to the ordinary football fan, when seen in terms of people and personalities. And Patrick Vieira was a dominant personality influencing the perception of the Arsenal brand, since he arrived in that crucible period of the 1996–97 season. Three startling changes of personality entered the Arsenal

ARSENAL

PATRICK VIEIRA

stage at that time: the rehabilitated Tony Adams and the almost simultaneous arrivals of Arsène Wenger and Patrick Vieira. And through a process that seems like alchemy, the essence of Arsenal remained the same, but the club and the brand was reformed into something that was newer, more glittering and more sophisticated.

At the start of that season, Arsenal fans were completely in the dark. It was if a fog had descended over the stadium to obscure what was happening inside, particularly off the pitch. Bruce Rioch had been removed as manager, Pat Rice took temporary charge of the team and a new manager would be appointed soon. The rumour was that the manager-to-be was Arsène Wenger: Arsène who? was the response. For contractual reasons his appointment could not be officially confirmed until his Japanese employers Grampus 8 released him. This would take several weeks.

In the meantime, the surest sign that Wenger was indeed manager came with the announcement that Arsenal had signed two French players, Remi Garde and Patrick Vieira. The names meant nothing to Arsenal fans. Vieira seemed the more significant signing because he cost £3.5 million and he was joining from AC Milan. He was young (just 20), had joined Milan from Cannes, and had played mainly for Milan's reserve team. It seemed an interesting signing but not one to get too excited about.

Towards the end of September, in a midweek game against Sheffield Wednesday, Arsenal fans had their first sighting of Patrick Vieira in an Arsenal shirt. Before the game we had seen and heard Arsène Wenger for the first time, on a video broadcast from Japan – the first in a continuing series of inaudible pre-match appearances from the boss. Vieira was on the substitutes' bench but, after about 20 minutes, he came on to replace the injured Ray Parlour. At this point Arsenal were 1–0 down and playing badly. Vieira came on and instantly gave meaning to a thousand football clichés. He was awesome. He took the game by the scruff of the neck. Arsenal ended up 4–1 winners and Highbury had a new hero.

Having grown accustomed to midfield players from the last days of the George Graham regime, Vieira's impact was refreshing. He was tall and lanky, he won tackles that shorter legs could never win and won balls in the air that smaller players could not reach. Having won the ball, he used it well, mainly with short passes that kept the player moving but also by surging forward with the ball at his feet. The spectacle of Vieira on the pitch – athletic, muscular, dynamic – brought a level of excitement that had become too rare in recent seasons. He won the fans' hearts in his first match and he consolidated that through his first season of stirring performances.

It was apparent that Vieira was Wenger's idea of Arsenal's future. The expectation was that the new manager would be ruthless with the old guard. Arsenal's strength at this time was its defence: Seaman in goal, Dixon, Adams, Bould, Keown, Winterburn as the back line. All players in their 30s and heading towards retirement. But Arsène Wenger assessed them, recognised their enduring qualities, changed their diet and exercise regimes, and gained extra years from each of them. No doubt they were helped defensively by the presence of Vieira in front of them, closing down the opponents' play and switching the ball efficiently to the other end of the pitch.

Patrick Vieira was born in Dakar, Senegal in June 1976. At the age of eight he moved to France with his mother and brother. They lived in Trappes, a rough suburb of Paris until Patrick's growing football prowess brought him attention. He was signed by Cannes, receiving recognition by the French national coaching system. He was also noticed by the manager of Monaco, just along the Riviera coast. Arsène Wenger noted the name and two years later, put the name forward to David Dein as the first signing he wished to make.

In the close season of 1997, Wenger made another important signing. He was now starting to shape his own team, while retaining the solid foundation of the English defence. The important signing was Emmanuelle Petit, recruited to be a midfield partner for Patrick Vieira. Other signings happened, ranging from relatively expensive stars like Marc Overmars to cheap but unknown players like Luis Boa Morte, Alberto Mendez and Christopher Wreh. Another young player,

Nicolas Anelka, was controversially poached from Paris St Germain. The new players were an exotic-sounding bunch, drawn from a wider world and using a deeper knowledge of football's international levels than Arsenal managers had ever displayed before. Not all the signings succeeded but all of them contributed something. Fans looked at each other when news came of a signing and they smiled 'Arsène knows'.

Play on the field was transformed too. With Vieira at the hub of the team, given even greater fluidity by the tactical awareness of Petit alongside him, the Arsenal team started to produce better football. It was also winning football. With a late, sustained surge in the second half of the season, Arsenal overtook Manchester United to win the League, and overcame Newcastle to win the FA Cup. Tony Adams was the captain, but Patrick Vieira was the most influential player on the pitch. At the end of the season there was little rest because the 1998 World Cup was held in France. With England's early elimination, Arsenal fans retained a real interest in the progress of the French team. There was an exciting but inconsistent player called Thierry Henry whom many noticed. But there were also Petit and Vieira, key players for 'les bleus'. In the final, already 2–0 and coasting against Brazil, France moved forward again in the last minutes. Vieira passed to Petit who slipped the ball in the net to make the final score 3–0 and win the World Cup. Arsenal fans cheered.

The winning French team was a rainbow team, containing players of many races from all parts of "greater France" – from islands in the Pacific, countries in Africa and small towns in France itself. In a country threatened by the rise of racism and Le Pen's National Front, it was significant that France had succeeded by uniting its races in a common cause. Almost without being aware of it happening, Arsenal was undergoing a similar transformation in perceptions. Arsenal had always been one of the most receptive clubs to black fans, attracted by black players like Paul Davis, David Rocastle and Ian Wright. Now the cosmopolitan mix of the Arsenal team was changing the way fans thought about their club. People decided that cosmopolitan, multiracial and diverse were good qualities to be associated with. Patrick Vieira was the obvious symbol, soon to be joined by Thierry Henry who would in time eclipse him in terms of cool.

But it was not just a matter of image. It was about winning and Vieira symbolised Arsenal's sheer will to win. His journalist friend Pierre Menes describes it like this. "Off the pitch, Patrick is the African, very cool and relaxed. On the pitch he is defined by his hatred of losing." Sometimes this seemed to go too far. Vieira was sent off regularly but not always (in Arsenal eyes) deservedly. Opposing players recognised his passion, knew that he had a short fuse, and succeeded in winding him up. Vieira got a reputation as a dirty player, and it became hard to escape. The reputation led to bookings and red cards, and these made him even more of a target for the next opponent and the next referee. This was no doubt particularly exasperating for Arsène Wenger who wanted his key man on the pitch. Over many seasons Wenger succeeded in calming Vieira down so that red cards became relative rarities and Vieira led a team that came top in the Fair Play table.

The team built around Vieira by Arsène Wenger continued to flourish. Between 1998 and 2005 Arsenal finished no lower than second in the Premiership. In 2002 they won another Double and, the following season, Vieira became Captain in succession to Tony Adams. This seemed a natural choice, particularly given Vieira's apparent commitment to Arsenal on the pitch. Yet it proved a controversial choice too, first because Vieira was a much less vocal captain than Adams. He led by example, but his encouraging effect on team mates sounded less apparent.

More importantly, people were forced to question Vieira's commitment by a regular series of well-reported temptations to join other clubs. First, in the close season of 2000, Vieira was linked with Juventus. Then it seemed like every summer he was a target for Real Madrid. In 2004, the situation became very serious. Vieira agonised for two months over Real Madrid's offer. It seemed he was in a state of mental torment. Madrid was attractive because they described him as the world's best in his position. He would also play alongside his national captain Zidane. And, of course, the money would be good. There was a snag in that, though. Real Madrid pay the most money to the most marketable players – these are the galacticos, and they include Zidane, Ronaldo and Beckham. The galacticos retain control of image rights, which means that they can earn fortunes through global marketing and merchandising on top of their enormous salaries. As Real Madrid develops as a global brand, the value of being a Madrid galactico becomes ever greater. However, Real Madrid's leaders did not see Vieira as a galactico and were unwilling to pay him what he wanted. This meant that his earning power would not be significantly higher at Madrid than at Arsenal (where he was the highest paid player). At the last minute too, Arsenal dug their heels in to stick to a transfer price of £23 million.

In the end, though, the decision to stay at Arsenal was Vieira's. He had spent the summer consulting those closest to him: Dennis Bergkamp, Thierry Henry, his partner Cheryl and his mother Mama Rose. They all left the decision to him. Deciding became impossible. It came down to pure emotion finally. Vieira loved living in London, he was idolised by the fans who sang his name with his own song. He felt at ease with the multicultural, metropolitan life in England, whereas Spain had shown a nasty streak of voluble racism directed at black players. He had become increasingly aware of responsibility to his native Africa, and established the Diambars Institute, a football and educational academy, in his birthplace Senegal. All these thoughts were pulling him in different directions. Eventually, two days before the first game of the 2004/05 season, Vieira called at Arsène Wenger's home. Expecting an emotional "thank you and goodbye", Wenger heard an equally emotional "I've decided to stay".

In the following days, the newspapers were full of Patrick Vieira proclaiming "I'm staying because I love Arsenal". But this was the fourth season in a row that Arsenal fans had been subjected to a similar saga. People were less ready to accept his words on trust. He had to prove himself again on the field, even though he had just captained Arsenal to the Premiership title and a record of going a whole season unbeaten. Arsenal fans have an overriding loyalty to the Arsenal itself. The club is always bigger than any player; the brand is bigger than any sub-brand. So, effectively, the challenge went down: show us what Arsenal means to you.

For most of the 2004/05 season Patrick Vieira did not rise to the challenge. He began the season injured, and the suspicion of injury lingered through the season: he seemed distracted, off the pace. He lost his steady midfield partner, the Brazilian Gilberto, to an injury that lasted most of the season. Gilberto's replacements were young and inexperienced, even if immensely talented: Flamini and Fabregas. Vieira found his true form only occasionally, mainly in the FA Cup, and Arsenal had a 'disappointing' season, finishing second in the League behind Chelsea. Most disappointing of all was another failed European Champions League campaign, the competition that most people at Arsenal now craved to win.

It was a sign of how far Arsenal had come during Vieira's then nine years at the club. Nine years is most of a footballer's career, so it seems slightly churlish of fans to question his commitment. Yet the Madrid saga had affected everyone deeply, most of all Vieira himself. It seemed that he spent most of the season coming to terms with his decision to stay. By the final matches the old dominance and fire seemed to be returning. The only hope of a trophy for Arsenal, having surrendered the League, was to beat arch-rivals Manchester United in the FA Cup Final.

It turned out to be the perfect ending. A forgettable game stayed 0–0 after 90 minutes and extra time. Arsenal had one shot on goal, United had many. But there was a George Graham-like resilience about the team, especially the defence marshalled by the young Swiss Philippe Senderos. The game went to a penalty shoot-out. Lauren and Ljungberg scored for Arsenal, but Scholes missed for

8th April 2001 ARSENAL'S PATRICK VIEIRA SCORES AGAINST LONDON RIVAL TOTTENHAM HOTSPUR

United so Arsenal went ahead. Van Persie and Ashley Cole scored to keep Arsenal ahead. Keane scored for United to make it 4–4 with one penalty to go. Up stepped the captain, Patrick Vieira.

We looked at each other from the heights of the Millennium Stadium in Cardiff. We were remembering Vieira's penalty miss in the UEFA Cup Final against Galatasaray some years before. He is not a completely assured penalty taker, he is not one of those players who has total command of the ball when he kicks it. But he has will power. He stepped forward and powered the ball into the net, driven by his own will. His final kick of the game had won the Cup for Arsenal and it would be Patrick Vieira who would raise it to the Arsenal fans from the podium. It was the most fitting end to another chapter.

A new chapter began for Patrick Vieira in the 2005 close season. This time he was transferred to Juventus for 20 million euros. It seemed that the transfer was engineered by Arsenal. Despite the shock expressed by media and fans, Arsène Wenger's cool judgement was that Vieira's playing peak had passed, his value in terms of money and football was in decline. And no doubt, there was the thought that the captain, above all, needs to be totally committed to the club if the club is to 'win together'. There was no doubt a sense of betrayal that Vieira had urged Ashley Cole to go aggressively for more money in a new contract, and this led directly to the tapping-up saga with Chelsea.

So, in the end, Ashley Cole stayed, at least for another season. Patrick Vieira left, with the good wishes of the fans, to be replaced as captain by a player who had already become an Arsenal legend, Thierry Henry.

Patrick Vieira deserves the last words to be his own, though, saying as he walked out the door: "The fans were always fantastic to me and when I went to the training ground to say goodbye to everyone it was quite emotional. The medical staff, the office people, the kitchen staff, the chef, I know them all well and my relationship with them has been fantastic. It is just a special club."

And next?

Thierry Henry stands apart, one of the great footballers of all time and potentially a great captain. Certainly an attractive brand icon. Arsenal have had the best years of his career. But Arsenal fans believe they might have seen a future Arsenal captain and a legend in the making during the last weeks of the 2004/05 season. In the 119th minute of the Cup Final, having defended all game to keep Manchester United out, Philippe Senderos burst out of his own half with the ball at his feet. He drove at the heart of the United defence, forcing them back just when they wanted to come forward. That was the Arsenal spirit.

Philippe Senderos was born in 1986 in Switzerland to a Spanish father and a Serbian mother. He joined Arsenal in preference to Real Madrid, both Milan clubs, Manchester United and Bayern Munich. He thought he would learn more at Arsenal. He speaks five languages and will talk to you about religion, politics, philosophy and literature. He seems to represent everything that the 21st century Arsenal stands for yet is also the most natural successor to Tony Adams. There is a consistency of values, and it runs through the Arsenal captains who are brand icons.

Chapter 4

Seeing and believing

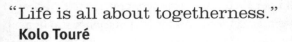

"Life is all about togetherness."
Kolo Touré

What is the Arsenal brand – what does it stand for? We can draw conclusions from our personal experience (Chapter 1), from history (Chapter 2) and from past and present players who stand as representatives (Chapter 3). The elements that make up the 'brand model' – mission, vision and values, or other ways of defining the essence of the brand – have never been publicly stated by Arsenal. To do so would invite derision in some quarters (from those who object to the commercialisation of football and its drift from amateur and/or working class roots). In other quarters it would invite disagreement. But disagreement and debate are two of football's great pleasures, so we will offer up our view of a brand model in that spirit.

Arsenal went through a process of brand definition before introducing a new logo in 2001. The brand consultancy 20|20 interviewed people in the club as the foundation of their research and proposed the following brand values: respect for people, a sense of belonging, a gentleman's club, stable and reliable, self-belief and resilience, open and innovative, a passion. These values went with a brand promise "winning the game".

Even though the process itself might be seen as controversial in some diehard quarters, we need to stress that for Arsenal to think in terms of its brand is simply good management. It needs to be done if Arsenal is to compete in marketing against its domestic and international rivals. And it needs to compete in marketing if it is to generate funds to buy the players who will compete on the pitch. Given that it needs to be done, Arsenal's management have gone about the task in a professional way when the populist approach might have been to invite a 'new logo' from the ranks of fans. Arsenal has at least recognised that the visual identity needs to be built on principles and values that are true to Arsenal and its vision of the future – even if, when it came to it, the management took the new logo without really using the brand principles to guide it any further. They relied on their own instinctive feel for the brand, for what it means to be Arsenal.

This makes it all the more necessary, in this book, to analyse what the brand's essence and values truly are. Because there is a brand there, it is understood intuitively by all those who come into contact with it. Indeed it is this understanding of the brand, not openly articulated, that attracts new fans and new generations of fans to Arsenal. No brands are more emotive than football brands. Loyalists of football brands usually decide early in life that 'this is my club' and then they stick to it through thick and thin. The brand – what the club really stands for in the minds of others – establishes and maintains a lasting relationship. People shape and live their lives according to the perceived code of the brand. 'Living the brand' is a concept far more meaningful when applied to a football fan than when, as it usually is, applied to an employee or consumer of a conventional business brand.

* * *

For the Premiership period – until the Premier League insisted from the start of the 2004–05 season on a uniform way to introduce all teams onto the pitch – Arsenal players made an entrance that became a distinctive element of their identity. Arsenal were the first and only team to run out onto the pitch, line up in the centre and wave to all four sides of the stadium, home and away. The eleven players would applaud the crowd, the crowd would applaud them, a unity of purpose was visibly established between the Arsenal team and its supporters.

Over the season 2003–04, during which Arsenal set a record of going unbeaten for the whole season of 38 games while winning the league, another refinement developed. Just before kick-off the captain Patrick Vieira would high-five every member of the team, then they would go into a huddle, arms over each other's shoulders. Asked about this, Robert Pires the French midfielder, revealed that the word spoken by everyone in that huddle was "together". An English word, spoken in English, by a team of many nations and many tongues.

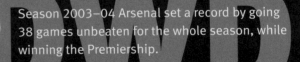

Season 2003–04 Arsenal set a record by going 38 games unbeaten for the whole season, while winning the Premiership.

ther

At the beginning of the following season, as they approached and surpassed the record for the longest-ever unbeaten run in English football, another ritual took place. A huddle at the end of the match signalled a collective resolve to continue the work into the next game. Then, at the beginning of every game (as other teams had now imitated the huddle) it became the practice for each member of the team to high-five and hug each of the others. What would the stiff-upper-lips of earlier eras have made of this? They might have frowned at the particular expression but understood the intention.

While these symbols were developing, Arsène Wenger kept his cool, stressing not only the team's exceptional footballing quality but also its sense of togetherness. "There is a camaraderie here that is very strong," he pointed out. In the same week Patrick Vieira rejected a big-money move to Real Madrid, the club with the greatest buying power in the world, and English defender Sol Campbell announced that he would sign a new contract with a pay cut to stay at Arsenal: "I have been in the game long enough to know that you can go chasing around trying to get the kind of feeling, spirit and togetherness we have at Arsenal and never succeed".

Exceptional team and exceptional times, reinforcing the sense that there is a brand, a strong idea of what Arsenal stands for, an idea that lives in the minds of its consumers and its representatives. Some people might think this a recent invention, as brands are generally (but wrongly) considered to be. Yet the qualities demonstrated by the team out on the pitch, the identity exemplified by the players, the identification felt by the fans – these are not marketing inventions but the result of many years of shaping. The Arsenal brand is strong and deep-rooted. Its effect on the minds and lives of those who pledge loyalty to it is fundamental and long-lasting. The sense of togetherness is tangible.

Way back in its early years, the Arsenal board of directors agreed on a club crest with a Latin motto. *Victoria concordia crescit*. As with most of these Latin tags most people give it little consideration, believing it to be an insignificant piece of mock-heraldry. Yet in this case it is worth thinking about because it comes close to representing the essence of the Arsenal brand. 'Victory grows through harmony' might be a literal translation. Or in a freer version, as in the title of this book, 'winning together'. The Latin motto actually points towards the core values of the Arsenal brand that lie at the heart of its continuing success.

* * *

So how might we define those values, built around the brand essence of winning together? As with any brand that creates a genuine emotional connection, people are important. A brand works best when its values create and exemplify stories that its adherents can relate to. To suggest such stories we need to use the words of real brand spokespeople and we need to go beyond the lazy, single-word definitions that too many brands have adopted in recent years.

The first value we suggest is exemplified by a quotation from Patrick Vieira:

"It is one of the great things about Arsenal that we have the strength and spirit to show courage in the face of adversity."

The first brand value is **Courage in the face of adversity.**

A second value, also supported by a quotation from a recent player, is **Loyalty to each other.** Robert Pires said:

"The attitude, the solidarity of a group, its force of character. In terms of Arsenal, that's what we are trying to do."

The third value is introduced by a quotation from Arsène Wenger.

"You always want to be positive because I believe, really deeply, in my side and when it doesn't work out as well as you think it should, you deal with it."

This gives us the third value **Positive about the future.**

Because the fourth value is almost a counterpoint to the third, it is appropriate to demonstrate it with another quotation from Arsène Wenger. These are words he spoke at the press conference to launch the 'historic' kit design that the team would wear in 2005–06, the final season at Highbury.

"I love the fact that the team will be wearing a home kit that is inspired by the first one ever worn at Highbury. It's not only a way of encapsulating more than 90 years of memories, it also takes us right back to when we started at this ground in 1913."

The fourth and final value is **Proud of our past.**

Perhaps there should be one other quotation to sum up the brand essence and values together. This comes from Thierry Henry, the Arsenal captain in 2005–06.

"Here everyone is pulling in the same direction but above all else there is an atmosphere I've never known before. We are all in the same boat. We laugh together. There is not a star. We are a true family, including the supporters."

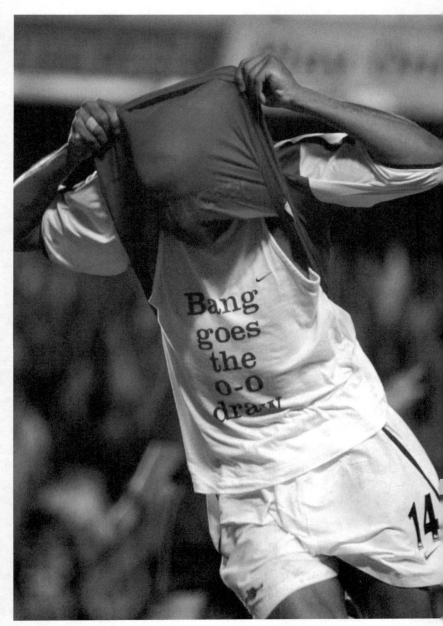

Arsenal's Thierry Henry covers his head with his shirt after scoring against
Liverpool, during the Premiership football match at Highbury (Arsenal won 2–0)

These brand values are rooted in the reality of the club. Football supporters identify with their team, in a sense they live their lives by the values they associate with the team. Although these values might not have been formally written down in these words before, they correspond to qualities Arsenal fans identify with through their team. What takes this beyond idle philosophising, away from the bland 'how to live your life' principles of new-age books and the Celestine Prophecies, are the stories constantly generated by actions on the football pitch. These stories reinforce the existing values we recognise in Arsenal, and they continue to build the legend that is the romantic heart of any football brand. And they should then be reflected in the visual elements of the identity, such as the logo.

* * *

Arsenal went through a process of brand definition before introducing a new logo in 2001.

The old badge had evolved over the years but not in a smooth evolution. The basic shape of the badge had been established as a shield, and we show here some of the process of evolution through the twentieth century. Important elements seem to be the shield shape, the motto and the cannon. The initials AFC have often been used rather than spelling out the name. Perhaps most important is the colour red. When the logo was developed into its current form, it was paraded around Highbury before a game and it was roundly booed on all sides. The general feeling among the fans was that the new logo had become too cartoon-like, losing much of the heritage, dignity and authority of the badge that it was replacing.

Several years on and the antagonism has died down. Comparing the new badge now with its predecessor, seen on photographs throughout this book, you can see that change had been necessary. The old logo looks quaintly old-fashioned; it does not reproduce well at a small scale; the details are fussy and mock-heraldic. The new logo is much simpler and works better in various media particularly

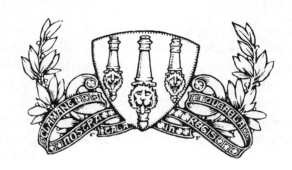

on television. It retains the essential cannon, a visual reference to the club's roots as Woolwich Arsenal, the munitions factory team. It also uses a typeface for 'Arsenal' that can be read with much greater clarity.

There was an obvious case for change and the Arsenal management pushed it through. Hindsight proves them right on the whole. Yet there was a practical reason for the change in logo that was never stated in public pronouncements. Arsenal knew that a more commercial age of marketing and merchandising was upon them. The club knew that it needed a logo that could be protected by copyright laws. It needed a new logo to establish a watertight copyright that would save the club time, effort and money. Only by doing so would it be able to protect its intellectual property rights on merchandise such as shirts. While taking to court small traders who sold unofficial shirts outside the ground, Arsenal was giving itself the weapons to sell its merchandise internationally and to make much more money as a result. Because, having created a new and distinctive logo, and having registered it, Arsenal was then in a position to protect its merchandise assets around the world. At least that is the theory. When China.com provided an official Arsenal website available to 100 million Chinese Internet users in summer 2005, the theory seemed to have been proved.

But we should not forget that identity is more than simply a logo. Having been around since 1886 Arsenal has acquired an accretion of many different identity elements, most of which are more familiar and important to Arsenal fans than the logo. Players of all clubs should be wary of the recent practice of kissing the badge on the team shirt. Kissing the badge has become a much imitated but devalued gesture to make. Too many players have kissed a badge one week then signed next week for an arch-rival. We worried when Thierry Henry scored against Chelsea then ran to the celebrating fans, badge raised to mouth. Oh no, we thought, is he going to be off?

With Henry perhaps we thought we need not worry, given what

seemed to be his genuine feeling for the club. But players might realise that the badge can be seen as a shallow symbol of identity. After all, fans were booing its new incarnation not too long ago.

Important elements of Arsenal's identity are names and colours. The name has aspects that are unique to Arsenal – or the Arsenal as the proudest and most diehard of fans would say. The name has its roots in the club's origins that also led to the secondary, semi-official nickname Gunners. The Gunners is a nickname actually used by members of the Arsenal family, whereas many football club nicknames exist only in the pages of tabloid newspapers and on Ceefax screens. From Gunner is derived the more recent and definitely unofficial name Gooner. The status of the name Gooner can be gauged by the position of the fanzine *The Gooner* as the most successful and the most long-lived – *The Gooner* was first published in 1987. The chant 'Oh to be a Gooner' has become one of the most popular (and one of the few definitely owned by Arsenal fans and not shared with other clubs). There was pleasure too in singing 'Sol's a Gooner' when Sol Campbell defected from arch-rivals Spurs.

Names are obviously important because they provide the basis for shouts and chants of encouragement at a football match. The shorter the better for these purposes. Longer names inevitably need to be shortened – to Juve for example, or Man U or the generic United.

Colour is an essential aspect of any football club's identity. *'Come on you Reds'* makes clear whose side you are on. Different shirt colours provide a way for players and fans to play and watch the game more easily. Arsenal wear red shirts, and they have done since they gained their first shirts, almost as an act of charity, from Nottingham Forest soon after the club was founded in the 1880s. The shirts were traditionally all red, a fact that had faded from everyday knowledge until the revival of the 1913 shirt for the final season at Highbury. To most people the Arsenal shirt tradition is red with a twist – white sleeves. The combination is unique in the highest division of English football, and has been since it was introduced

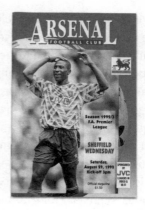

in the 1930s. The fact that a new shirt and unprecedented success went together meant that an unshakeable tradition was established. Change it at your peril. It did not work for Billy Wright in 1964 when he was trying to escape the 'burden' of the club's successful past by changing from shirts with white sleeves back to all-red.

There is, though a much greater license to change the secondary colours, particularly the away shirt. Blue and yellow have been the commonest combinations, but Arsenal have occasionally strayed into gold, even a touch of green. The proportions of blue to yellow are infinitely flexible, at the whim of next season's shirt designer from Nike (or whichever brand has the shirt contract at the time). On the whole this works. It allows for fashion changes, as long as the red and white combination stays in place for the main colours.

In recent years numbers have gained a talismanic value. The association of certain players with particular numbers has been a strong feature of football marketing. As fans buying the team shirt can then pay extra to have an individual name and number added, the marketing attraction is obvious. Some numbers become so strongly linked to certain players that the number is effectively 'retired'. When Tony Adams finished playing, the number 6 shirt was not adopted by another player. Even Sol Campbell, an England centre-back, felt uncomfortable at the thought – so he stuck to number 23 (a famous number, in the sporting world, worn originally by basketball star Michael Jordan, and now by David Beckham at Real Madrid). Some players get attached to their original squad numbers, perhaps given to them as a youth player getting a first chance to play for the first team. Kolo Touré, for example, has stuck with number 28 and it is now hard to imagine him with a different number on his back. And the number 14 has become synonymous with Thierry Henry at Arsenal.

In many ways this is the stuff of football trivia. Yet it is also an inextricable part of football's mythology. It is what feeds the obsessions of obsessive fans. While acknowledging the need to put away childish things, fans never want to lose the link to the inner

child that football keeps young. It is why visual identity is such a
powerful element of a football brand. Of course, 'identity' does
exactly what the word suggests. It enables supporters to identify
with their team, through the badge, the colours and other visual
manifestations of the brand. And through these to a deeply felt, but
rarely articulated, understanding of the values that are embodied
by the brand.

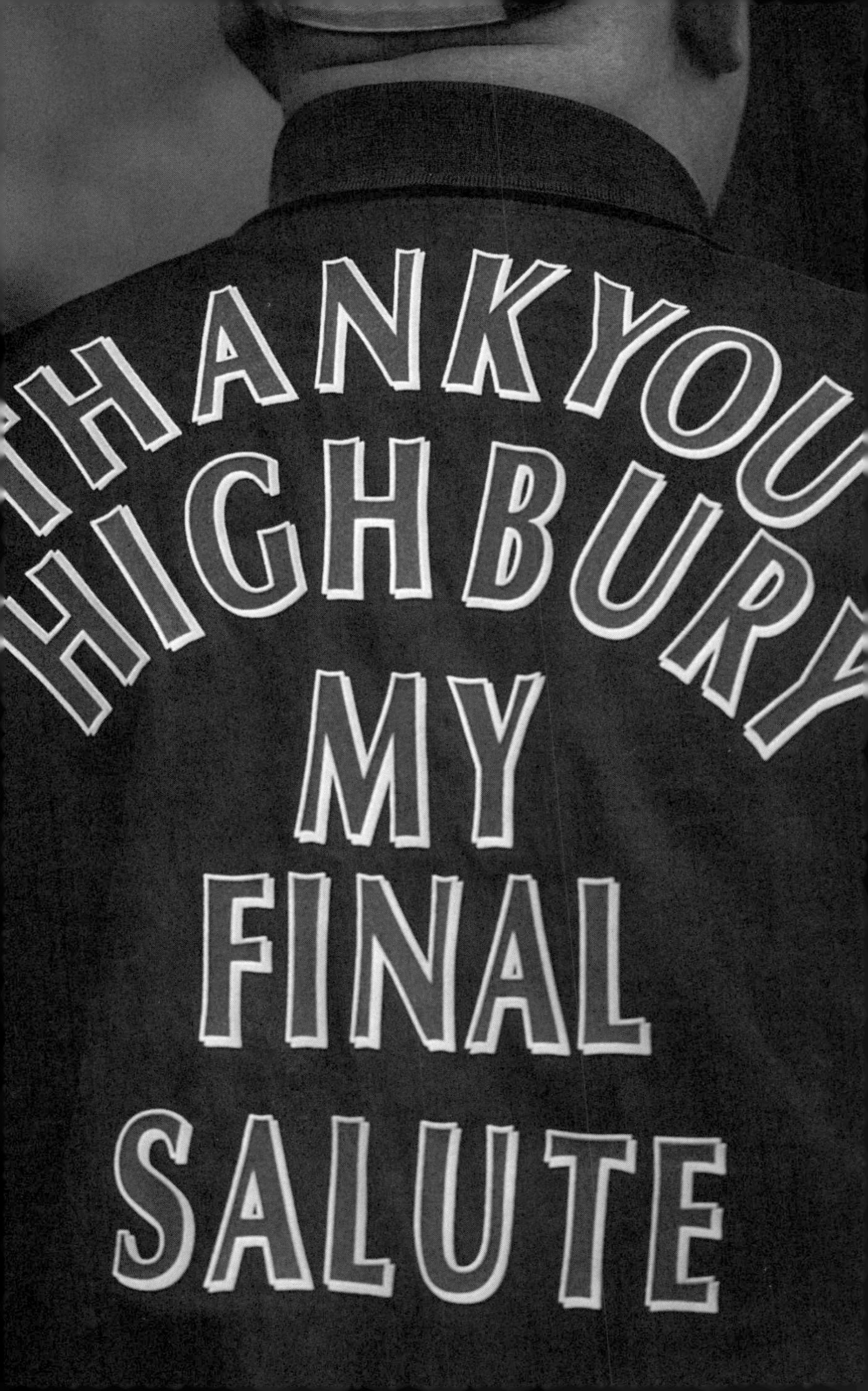
HANKYOU
HIGHBURY
MY
FINAL
SALUTE

The business of branding

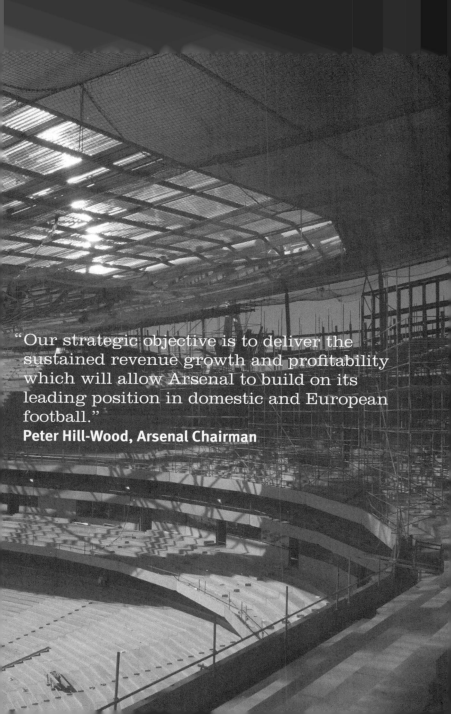

"Our strategic objective is to deliver the sustained revenue growth and profitability which will allow Arsenal to build on its leading position in domestic and European football."
Peter Hill-Wood, Arsenal Chairman

In 1992 football in England changed more dramatically than at any other time in its history. The Premiership was born, in response to the financial temptations of Sky TV. As a result football was changed worldwide too. A small league that had grown weaker from many years of enforced exclusion from European competition now grew bigger and bigger, richer and richer. Within 10 years the Premiership was alongside Serie A in Italy and Primera Liga in Spain as the three leading football leagues in the world.

Television gave them this position. When Sky first injected large amounts of cash into the English game, the main concern was that many people would be unable to afford Sky subscriptions and football would disappear from terrestrial TV. Deals were struck with BBC and ITV to keep some football (particularly Saturday night highlights) on licence-fee funded television. But no one seemed too concerned that unprecedented amounts of money would change the nature of the game itself. In fact, in the early days of the Premiership, the main concerns (fans' resentment and envy) were that a little club like Blackburn had achieved success thanks to the millions invested in new players by a local businessman, Jack Walker.

This now seems parochial. Jack's millions helped win Blackburn the Premiership title in 1994–95 but after that the real money rose to the top. Manchester United monopolised the Premiership's early years. Through their success they gained more TV coverage, gaining more TV money as a result. From their point of view it was a virtuous circle, but it became clear that the Premiership's structure based on TV money was distorting the competition. The biggest club bought the best players, and it was hard for others to challenge. Liverpool were in decline, Leeds were spending beyond their means, Chelsea had false expectations of grandeur before the Russian roubles gushed in. Previous 'Big Five' clubs like Everton and Spurs were floundering. The only team to challenge Manchester United's domination was Arsenal, even though the gap in financial resources remained vast.

Arsenal won the Premiership in 1998, 2002 and 2004. Since Arsène Wenger's first full season in 1997–98 Arsenal have not finished outside the top two of the Premiership, and they have also won the FA Cup four times. The early monopoly by Manchester United turned into a duopoly with Arsenal and Manchester United sharing the major honours until Chelsea, bolstered by Abramovich's money, won the Premiership in 2005. In the same season Liverpool won the European Champions League. So it now appeared that there were four teams equipped to slug it out at the top of English football and in European competition. Except that the rise of Chelsea, "a financially doped club" as Arsène Wenger put it, has been fuelled by financial resources beyond the reach of every other club. A financial gulf now exists between Chelsea and the rest. But there is no doubt that each of these four English clubs has ambitions to be a global brand.

Arsenal's ambition was made clear to us in a business conversation with David Dein in 1998 while one of the authors was at Interbrand. We were talking about Arsenal's determination to build a brand that would compete against the likes of Real Madrid and AC Milan, as well as Manchester United. At the time Arsenal had chosen to play their European games at Wembley. The obvious reason for this was the difference in ground capacity – Highbury's 38,000 versus Wembley's 74,000. But it was also a way of testing the scale of Arsenal's customer base and the flexibility of its brand loyalty. Fans filled Wembley for every European match. The lesson was that Arsenal could fill a larger stadium than Highbury for domestic matches too. The hunt for a new stadium began in earnest. This required both belief in the power of the Arsenal brand and a capacity for visionary risk-taking. Many Arsenal fans had their doubts; most football commentators were sceptical. But the Arsenal board drew up its business plans and took brave decisions.

This is unusual in English football. *State of the game*, a study by Birkbeck College in 2004, revealed that only 62% of clubs have business plans that look more than one year ahead – beyond the end of the season. Even the one year business plan is no doubt hedged with wide variables depending on success or failure, trophies or relegation. Football club management has been slow to adopt conventional business principles, arguing that this is no conventional business. Indeed the football business is like business taken to an extreme, with rewards and penalties exaggerated for success or failure. You achieve success, you gain money, you spend it. Or you lose it trying to gain more instant success. Sir Alan Sugar, chairman of Tottenham, called it "the prune juice effect" – whatever goes in, quickly comes straight out again.

The brand can be a source of relative stability in this situation, as long as it remains focused around the core of the business. When football club directors start seeing £ signs instead of goal lines, they get carried away by possibilities beyond their expertise. It can be a swift way to end up buried under debt, as Leeds United did, or indeed Chelsea. It's easy to forget that Chelsea, believing that Chelsea Village could be a leisure and pleasure shopping complex, with a football pitch attached, came to the brink of bankruptcy before Roman Abramovich stepped in. And, by stepping in with millions of roubles, converted into pounds and euros, he emphasised again that football is seldom played to the normal commercial rules of business.

So, with the brand, keep it focused on the core business of football. That will attract valuable brand associations and sponsorship money. And it will help to sell merchandise such as replica shirts. There is a profitable medium between a pure and simple football-only business and a hotels and leisure conglomerate.

At times in recent years, on paper at least, Arsenal have seemed to be too removed from a pure football business. While the core activity on the pitch has been going well, the business has been unable to take full advantage because of the need for a bigger stadium. The search for and eventual decision to go ahead with the new stadium in Ashburton Grove has also turned Arsenal into a property company. In the long term profits will flow from this. In the short term the team itself has been subjected to enormous financial constraints that Arsène Wenger has had to manage his way around

with extraordinary skill. No other manager has achieved such a high return on investment from the players bought and sold over the last ten years. As the *Guardian* journalist Kevin McCarra put it: "Whereas Chelsea and Manchester United have fortunes at their disposal, Arsenal will be funded purely by the wealth of Wenger's imagination."

This relative impoverishment has been factored into Arsenal's planning. Large transfer funds will not be available until revenue from the new stadium starts flowing. Interviewed in March 2005, Arsène Wenger said: "For a period we will not be able to compete in the transfer market. That is why we prepared the young players. There is a double advantage: the financial demands are not so high and you can give them the values of the club during the time they spend in the academy." He speaks as a football team manager with a rare understanding of business – he is, after all, one of a very select band of managers with an Economics degree – but also as a brand manager. He sees the positive benefits of players understanding and living the values of the club.

But, after 2006, when the new stadium starts to be less of a financial drain, the outlook for Arsenal could be transformed.

Changing the business of football

The Premiership and Sky TV changed the commercial realities of English football. The amounts of money involved were of a previously unknown scale. Inevitably clubs started to think bigger and more greedily. Beyond the English leagues were the European clubs, many of them seeing themselves as super-clubs deserving to be placed in a higher league altogether. Fourteen of these clubs formed themselves into a grouping called G-14 in 2000, and the objectives of G-14 were to look after the interests of its members in the development of international club football. Among its original members were Real Madrid, Juventus, AC Milan, Barcelona and

Manchester United. Arsenal were not included in the original G-14 but made their way into an expanded group of 18 two years later.

G-14 was significant not for any achievements – no European league has yet come about, yet – but for the fact of its existence. It showed that the bigger European clubs were planning for growth, and that growth might involve a radical restructuring of the game at the highest level. If it has not happened yet, we suspect that this is because of conflicting self-interest within the group and the realisation that such change might be a marketing disaster. Because, belatedly, football clubs have realised that there is such a thing as marketing, even if few of them yet use its disciplines to any great effect.

Football discovered marketing in the 1990s, and Sky TV had much to do with it. Until that point, and to an extent since, many of the most basic principles of marketing could be ignored by football clubs. They simply relied on meeting the most fundamental needs of an audience – giving access to a 90-minute football match with minimal amenities. The audience was made up of fans, not customers, and no matter what you did they always seemed to come back for more. Churn is a marketing term used to describe a high turnover of customers. Many brands have very shallow roots – mobile phone companies, cable and broadcasting services, dotcoms, for example. Loyalty is only on the surface of these brands. Customers feel little loyalty to the brand and switch to a different one as soon as a more attractive offer appears. How these brands must envy football teams. There is remarkably little churn among football fans – generally the team you support in childhood is the team you support forever, through thick and thin. As the T-shirt says: "Gooner for life."

The trick for football clubs is going to be maintaining and building future audiences by treating them as customers as well as fans. Branding points any business in that direction. By taking the brand essence as "winning together" and thinking through what that really means, Arsenal will be able to build a better, more creative

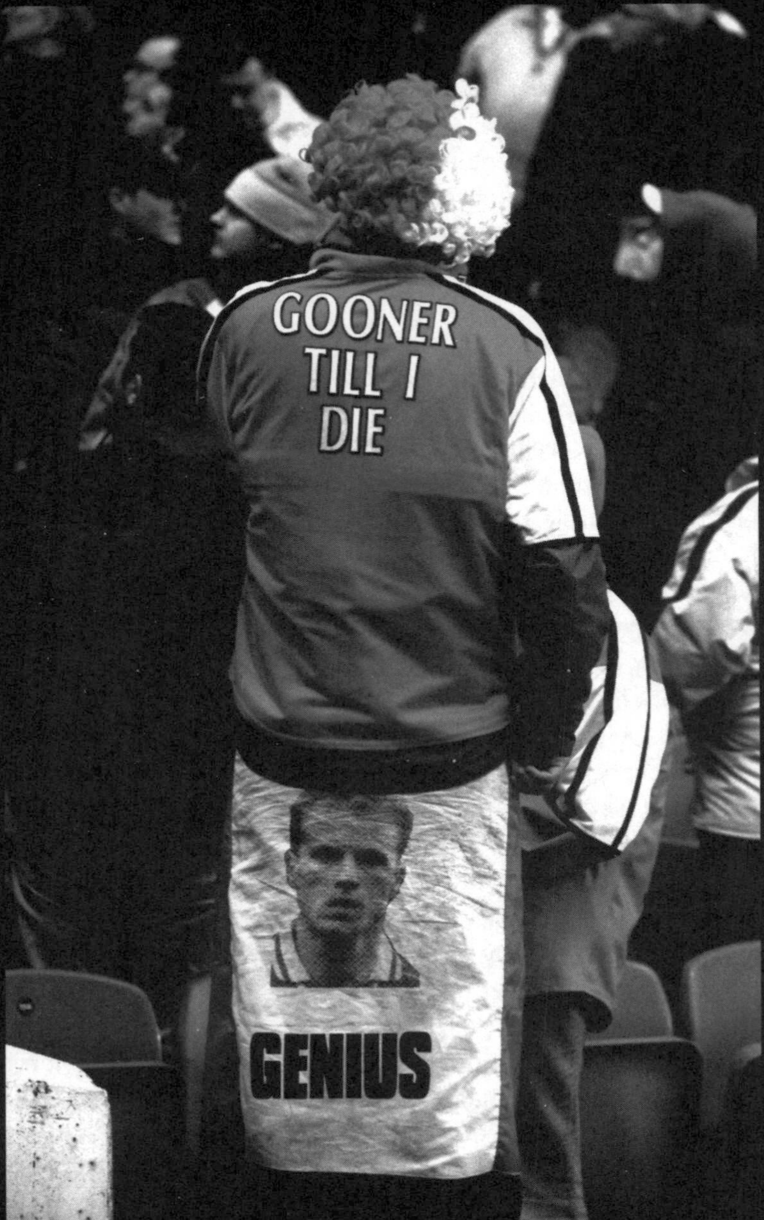
GOONER
TILL I
DIE
GENIUS

relationship with its fans/customers. And it has been fortunate that the stadium project has forced a lot of the necessary thinking to be done. Knowing that a new 60,000 capacity stadium will need to be filled, Arsenal started analysing its fans and working out how best to reach them.

The word 'members' began to be used to describe those who had made some form of financial commitment to the club (simply by buying tickets for matches). An expensive-looking pack was sent out to members of "The Arsenal" at the start of the 2004/5 season. Members were defined by a number of different categories. There were more than 100,000 members, including 21,161 Gold members (season ticket holders); 23,410 Silver members (ticket registration scheme members); 14,494 Junior Gunners; and the rest Red members (waiting list for tickets). This gave the basis for the marketing plan and also informed the plans for the new stadium.

Initial but unofficial projections for future revenue show that the stadium will take Arsenal onto a new playing field in more ways than one. The fact is that very little ever officially emerges from Arsenal on the finances of the club. Transfer fees are always 'undisclosed' while every other club is much more specific about the sums involved. It stems from tradition and from the fact that the ownership of the club is in the hands of a few people who make up the Board. But it seems clear that the match day revenues from the new stadium will significantly increase Arsenal's turnover.

There will be five main revenue streams from people paying to watch games. Club Level has been heavily marketed to existing season ticket holders as a way to 'trade up' and get the best view in the new stadium. With nearly 7,000 seats available at this level, the annual revenue will be something like £18 million. The second stream will be from 150 boxes, ranging in price from £65,000 to £150,000. Players such as Thierry Henry and Dennis Bergkamp are reported to have bought boxes, setting aside a week or two's salary. The expected revenue from the boxes is about £14 million. These figures, of course, are dependent on Arsenal selling all the available spaces in these levels, but the club has been issuing positive noises. At the beginning of the 2005/06 season Arsène Wenger said: "At one stage I thought it looked crazy. The capacity of 60,000 seemed a lot, but now I believe we will sell out every week and with a really great side I think we would get even more people, so maybe 60,000 looks too small."

These are bullish comments from a naturally cautious man, so there seems a genuine air of confidence about the new stadium's pulling power. But the two categories we have mentioned so far – Club Level and boxes – provide seats for fewer than 10,000 people and revenue of £32 million. Arsenal's current match day revenue from Highbury is £33 million, so money earned from selling the 50,000 'ordinary' tickets in Ashburton Grove will be additional to historic income levels. There is one more 'special' level of membership, the Diamond Club. Diamond Club members will pay £12,500 to see each game in a state of some luxury and no doubt the opportunity to discuss the ins and outs of the stock market at half-time. The bulk of tickets, though, 51,000 of them, are offered first to existing members of The Arsenal in either the Upper or Lower tiers of the new stadium. Guarantees have been given that season tickets will be sold to existing members at 'comparable prices' and that seems to be the case, at least for the first season. The likely impact on finances is £30 million from tickets in the upper tier, and £18 million in the lower tier – giving a total for the stadium of £81 million.

After several years of selling out Highbury's capacity of 38,000 for each match, it seems that there has been a genuine unfulfilled demand for tickets. Playing European games at Wembley tested that theory. The new stadium looks likely to prove it – and perhaps, as Arsène Wenger suggests, the 60,000 capacity will not be enough. The more people who come through the gates, of course, the more opportunities there are to sell extra products and services. A figure of £10 million for catering and programme sales in the new stadium looks achievable. Even with the cost of repaying the investment in the stadium – likely to be interest charges of £18 million per year – there should be a significant increase in profit.

These figures will send Arsenal soaring up the Deloitte table of the world's richest clubs, likely to be dominated by English clubs in the near future. But a big gap gets bigger every year between the top English teams and the other clubs that make up the Premiership. Arsenal are able to charge two or three times as much for a season ticket as, say, a club like Bolton that finishes in the top six of the Premiership and qualifies for Europe. Partly it's to do with geography and demographics – a wealthier catchment area in London – but part of it is do with the brand, the perception of value.

Deloitte Football Money League			2003–04 Season
			Income £m
1	(1)	Manchester United	171.5
2	(4)	Real Madrid	156.3
3	(3)	Milan	147.2
4	(10)	Chelsea	143.7
5	(2)	Juventus	142.4
6	(7)	Arsenal	115.0
7	(13)	Barcelona	112.0
8	(6)	Internazionale	110.3
9	(5)	Bayern Munich	110.1
10	(8)	Liverpool	92.3

The value of the brand

What, then, is the value of the Arsenal brand? It seemed a good question to put to Nick Liddell who specialises in brand valuation at Interbrand, the leading international brand consultancy. After a couple of weeks of investigation he came back with a surprising answer. The value of the Arsenal brand is zero. What? Why? "In order to have positive brand value you not only have to turn a profit, but

that profit has to be substantial enough to cover the opportunity cost of your tangible working capital. Because Arsenal's core operating profit is highly unlikely to reach over 10% of its turnover, I don't believe the club is going to be able to make enough money to cover the imputed rental charge against its tangible assets – a large proportion of which is taken up by the new stadium. If the club did manage to achieve sufficient profitability to cover its required return on tangible working capital, then the value of the brand could be high. In addition to strong profitability, valuable brands are characterised by a high role of brand in generating earnings, as well as by sufficient brand strength to ensure that brand-related earnings are stable in the future."

Nick Liddell's points apply to just about any football club, not just to Arsenal. It reinforces the point that football is a business like no other, often causing accountants to raise their eyebrows in disbelief. The underlying point he makes is that there is a strong brand there, but it is impossible to assign it a real figure on the balance sheet, as you could do with a more conventional business. The levels of debt are simply too high for an objective brand valuation but this will not necessarily prevent some clubs assigning a notional valuation of their own.

Nick's conclusion was: "The overall picture is of a brand that is important in generating revenues, but which could do more to add stability to the business by looking at how companies in other sectors manage their brands." Perhaps this is now part of football's attraction for businessmen like Malcolm Glazer and Roman Abramovich – they look at football from a business point of view and see its undeveloped business potential. In August 2005 Media Sport Investment, a consortium led by Kia Joorabchian, was looking for an English club to buy, having already bought and transformed Corinthians in Brazil. Figures were bandied about for West Ham, in particular. The consortium had focused on West Ham because it could be bought for "£60 million of equity plus £30 million for debts". A spokesman said: "Chelsea is not for sale, Aston Villa are talking about £78 million, Newcastle would want £200 million to take the club private. Tottenham also want £200 million and Arsenal would be £400 million at least."

Malcolm Glazer bought Manchester United for £790 million which many financial observers thought was too high a price. But we have to presume that Glazer knows what he is doing and even if, according to accountants, Manchester United's valuation is speculative, it seems clear that the main value to Glazer is in the brand itself. This was acknowledged by Joe McLean, a football finance expert at accountants Grant Thornton: "The Glazers are exploiting the United brand overseas through better marketing, especially in Asia and North America, as the surest way to make money."

The brand is a football club's greatest underused asset. Gate revenues provide a bedrock of (relatively forecastable) income, but clubs make additional money from three areas that are directly related to the strength of the product on the pitch and the brand itself. These areas are TV and broadcasting rights, merchandising and sponsorship. And each of these needs to operate in an international marketplace. Clubs might be based in the bricks and mortar of London, Manchester or Madrid, but they live as dreams in all other parts of the world that engage with the experience.

The main way that they do this is through TV and other remote communications, including the Internet and mobile phones. TV has been the fuel of football's commercial development over the last twenty years. Arsenal's financial results in 2003–04 included broadcasting income of £59.8 million compared with gate receipts of £33.8 million. While no one would ever contemplate broadcasting matches from empty stadiums, the reality is clear that TV money matters more to the club than money through the gate. And TV money is the reason why European competition has become such a necessary part of the running of a football club. Arsenal earned £19.3 million from Champions League broadcasting in that season, for reaching the quarter finals of the competition. In the following season, reaching only the last 16, income dropped. But the stakes are higher now. Football has sold more and more of its soul, as well as its family silver, to TV. Future income is less certain, partly because of the changing nature of the technology and partly because of concerns, expressed by David Dein, about "saturation coverage".

Champions League TV money, 2004–05	
1 Liverpool	£20.5m (winners)
2 Chelsea	£18.8m (last 4)
3 AC Milan	£17.5m (runners up)
4 Arsenal	£15.7m (last 16)
8 Manchester United	£10m (last 16)
19 Celtic	£7m (group stage)

Arsenal's relative lack of success in Europe has cost them financially but perhaps not as much as might have been imagined. They remain a team that people want to watch and that influences broadcasters. The real difference is between the teams that are in the Champions League and those who are not. In terms of making money, it is popularity that counts and increasing the number of people who are exposed to the brand and disposed to look favourably upon it.

Alex Fynn, a consultant who was involved in the creation of the Premier League, emphasises the increasing importance of TV money. "There are three key sources of income – matchday revenues, commercial income and broadcasting money. Broadcast comes with no costs attached. Income from broadcast is also a direct result of success on the pitch. The more successful you are in the Premier League, the more you earn from Sky. But, more importantly, the more you earn from UEFA because the lion's share of their money goes to the richest market, which is the UK. And, within that, the biggest share goes to the Premiership champions."

Other TV and new media developments are emphasising the importance of a successful brand in generating income. Every Arsenal game is now sold and broadcast live in Scandinavia.

The Premiership allows clubs to sell programme blocks (three hours each) to overseas markets such as the Middle East. These blocks include a current game, topped and tailed with preview and review material. This becomes the equivalent of a TV channel. And, although Arsenal has not gone the route of the dedicated channel (unlike

Arsenal went to court to force out unofficial merchandise

Manchester United and Chelsea), its website is now rich in content. With the spread of broadband, the boundaries between TV and Internet are blurring, and in future years we will watch more TV on our computer screens. Arsenal's investment in its website should overcome any perceived weakness in not having its own TV channel. As the brand's website is more generally available than niche regional TV channels, it is actually a more democratic form of marketing – and possibly a more reliable indicator of popularity.

A visible sign of such popularity is the number of replica shirts sold, and this is often cited as the prime example of rapaciousness by football's business men. Shirt sales are significant but manufacturing companies have the major influence over pricing. Arsenal's shirt manufacturer is Nike and the deal with Nike in 2004 will raise £55 million for Arsenal over seven years. Arsenal's retail operation is relatively puny and does not leave major retailers looking on in envy. No doubt this is another area, along with catering, business and conference facilities, that will be developed in the new stadium.

You can tell a lot about a brand from the company it keeps. In football much of that company comes in the form of sponsorship. Granada (now ITV) has invested in Arsenal in return for certain broadcasting and publishing rights, reemphasising the vital role of football in the communications world based on digital technology. When the stadium financing was agreed in October 2004, Granada released £30 million of investment to the club – a useful sum in cash-strapped times. The shirt sponsorship deal has been with O_2, the mobile phone operator, for some years. It increased from £2 million to £3 million in 2005 but this is much less than the figures achieved by Chelsea and Manchester United with their latest shirt sponsorship deals. But part of the value that was seen in the arrangement with O_2 was the association with and entry into the mobile communications market. This seemed to offer possibilities to build relationships with younger generations of customers through the use of mobile phones and the technology converging around them.

The most significant sponsorship deal has been for the naming rights of the new stadium at Ashburton Grove. Most Arsenal fans would have preferred to keep the name untainted by a commercial deal. Naming the stadium might have been a popular competition for the fans and New Highbury or the Wenger Stadium would have been among the front-runners. But if you accept that you are running a business and that you own a valuable property (both the physical and intellectual asset), then money raised by selling the naming rights can be used to do what the fans want – ensure future success on the pitch. It happens that this coincides completely with everyone's interest, the board's, the fans', the sponsor's. So while there was apprehension and a little resentment when Arsenal appointed Envision to secure the naming sponsorship deal, there was acceptance when the deed was done. And, no doubt, a fair amount of bloody-minded "I'm still going to say I'm off to the Arsenal".

When 'Emirates Stadium' was announced, the greatest doubt and the heaviest irony was that Emirates Airlines had sponsored Chelsea's shirts for several years. But there was satisfaction in realising too that Emirates wanted an association with brand qualities that were greater than sheer financial power. Emirates presumably saw the value of subtler associations coming from the relationship with the Arsenal brand. People respond to imagination and there will be imaginative opportunities to explore with Emirates that more homespun sponsorship deals might not realise. When bmi, for example, announced a deal in 2004 to be the 'official airline of Arsenal' (handy for all those European away matches), the justification for the partnership seemed a typical case of unimaginative 'brandspeak': "The sense of history, strength and achievement is there as a common thread that links our two brands and this partnership can only breed one thing as a result – success."

The Emirates sponsorship of the stadium was on a different level. It guaranteed £90 million (£100 million at 'present value') to cover the stadium naming rights for 15 years and shirt rights for 8 years from 2006. The added attraction, perhaps the main attraction for the board, was that the payment was front-loaded so that cash flow would be improved in the early years when stadium financing costs were at the highest. The financial attraction was clear but a doubt remained about Emirates itself. Why not a major global brand like Sony or Nike? some asked. Perhaps the best response to this was given in the Letters page of *The Gooner* by a fan called Michael Brooks who works in the airlines business. "I'm biased towards sponsorship of Arsenal by a highly respected, global airline rather than a dodgy mobile phone company or a soft drink of dubious reputation. In surveys worldwide, Emirates Airlines is rated exceptionally well; certainly on a par with the original 'world favourite' – Singapore Airlines – and certainly better regarded than our own dear British Airways. Indeed, as an indication of the size and strength of Emirates, they carry more long-haul passengers than BA."

The point Michael Brooks then went on to develop was about the potential for Arsenal to become a worldwide brand. An Arsenal shop at Dubai International airport? And elsewhere around the world. In-flight entertainment? All valid possibilities to be explored but even more imaginative ideas might be needed. There is a big issue to be faced by football brands seeking to be global brands and to exploit their franchises through other business operations. Manchester United, for example, started opening up RedCafés in south-east Asia, then rapidly brought them to a halt. Brands need to think through what will really work. Simply saying "We're a global brand" is not a licence to print money. You have to work at it and be clever. There is a big question about whether partisan brands (which football brands are) can ever reach successfully beyond the zones of their partisanship. Put simply, no Arsenal fan would set foot inside a RedCafé operated by Manchester United – and no doubt the reverse is true too.

Managing the brand

An uncomfortable fact for football management is that the relationship between club and players has fundamentally changed. Clubs are still coming to terms with the Bosman ruling and fearful that further changes could shift the balance of power even more in favour of the player. Bosman removed some feudal aspects from transfer activity and player contracts, and in doing so it made players more aware of their commercial power. Sportsmen and sportswomen have been used to endorse products in advertising for decades. For Denis Compton, 'the Brylcreem boy' in the 1950s, the advertising money was a useful addition to his meagre incomes playing football for Arsenal and cricket for England. Today both footballing incomes and advertising fees are higher than the Denis Compton generation might ever have dreamed about. A modern football player's agent has a role to play in negotiating the basic contract and in managing and exploiting the player brand. A recognition that players are brands in their own right has led Real Madrid to a policy of favouring galacticos, star players with commercial power.

The trick is in establishing the balance between the club brand and the various player brands within the club's framework. The players are media-savvy and they have a high valuation of their own worth. They know that they are brand icons for Arsenal (or for whichever club) and they employ agents not just to boost their salaries but to do that through gaining the maximum advantage from their individual brands. Realising that the clubs have used them to bolster the club brand, elite footballers worldwide are haggling over their image rights. But as Andy Milligan wrote in *Brand it like Beckham*: "Despite all the hype that surrounds brands and branding, the law of customer demand reigns supreme: if you don't have something worth buying, people won't buy it." No matter how seductive Freddie Ljungberg might look to men and women in his Calvin Klein underwear, no matter how cute Robert Pires looks in his Puma shoes, no matter how much Sol Campbell aspires to be a lifestyle brand, there has been only one superstar brand at Arsenal in the Premiership period.

Thierry Henry achieved this status because of his unique combination of brilliance on the pitch and his ability to be the embodiment of cool off the pitch and in advertising. The phrase 'Va-va-voom' seemed to have been invented for him alone in Renault advertising. The image portrayed by Henry in such advertising – and in other good performances for other brands – had made him an effective brand ambassador for Arsenal itself. There is no doubt that Henry and Arsenal worked synergistically to grow each other's brands internationally. Such commercial power, combined with his playing ability, made Henry an object of desire for many teams. If he chose to leave it would be impossible for Arsenal to resist, hard though they would try.

27th November 2002 THIERRY HENRY SALUTES THE ARSENAL AFTER SCORING HIS FIRST GOAL DURING ARSENAL'S 3–1 VICTORY OVER ROMA, AT THE OLYMPIC STADIUM, ROME, ITALY

Clearly brands have the power to make money and to sell products. They influence people and they can change minds and behaviour. That is not necessarily a sinister objective, and football players often refer to their responsibilities as role models. Brands can be a force for good and football brands can (and should) play an increasing role in using their power to benefit society. 'Arsenal in the Community' is a suitably modest name for a quiet activity that has been running since 1985. Few Arsenal fans know much about it but it has been able to benefit a large number of worthy causes over the last twenty years and more. There are the expected schemes, like soccer schools, that run locally and increasingly, internationally. Projects in Israel, the Ukraine and South Africa, among others, take the Arsenal name and a love of football to countries that are off the beaten track for most football clubs.

The community programme becomes more interesting, though, when it uses the power of the Arsenal brand and football itself to influence young people towards education and social inclusion. Arsenal runs a Study Support Centre in Islington, as a joint venture between the club, the local education department and the government. More than 5,000 students have attended after-school courses in literacy, numeracy and computer skills in five years. Players visit the Centre to give an Arsenal presence and to encourage the students. There are many other schemes that also involve Arsenal in the education system.

There are other projects that aim to engage disaffected youngsters through contact with Arsenal and through football. Arsenal Positive Futures began in 2004. This is a programme funded by the Home Office with the support of other government departments relating to sport and education. The project concentrates on three local estates, giving 10–19 year-olds the opportunity to take part in coaching sessions and football tournaments. An educational element persuades the youngsters towards learning and employment opportunities. And there is no doubt that for many youngsters, there is greater trust in activities offered by the Arsenal brand than by the more official establishment. As David Conn, author of *The Beautiful Game? Searching for the Soul of Football*, says: "Football can have a major role in helping young people find a way out of their problems. The professional clubs have kudos and credibility with young people, who are often cynical and mistrustful of authority. It should not be so outlandish an idea for the clubs to reconsider themselves as social institutions. They are sports clubs. That ought to mean more than showbusiness."

The challenge for Arsenal is to develop its brand as a force for commercial *and* social development. For the harder-nosed business people out there, these two aspects need not be completely separated. Indeed each reinforces the other. If Arsenal were to focus single-mindedly on the money-making opportunities of its brand, to the exclusion of broader social responsibilities, it would in time run out of steam and influence. Brands need to be loved. Football brands have an incredible advantage over brands of other kinds. They arouse not just love but an obsessive, forgiving loyalty. That brings with it an equally strong responsibility.

Running a football club
Five models to follow (or not)

MODEL ONE

Secret society

Arsenal

Arsenal has always run its business in a very private way. The Eton-educated Hill-Wood family have had an influence at board level for the best part of a century. Arsenal shares are listed on the OFEX market for private companies, but most shares are in the hands of a few board members who control the club. Fans own small numbers of token shares.

Plus

More focused on objectives

Not subject to major external pressures

Minus

What's going on?

Depends on the commitment and quality of a few people

MODEL TWO

It's my party

Chelsea, Milan

Wealthy, powerful individuals – Abramovich and Berlusconi – run the clubs as personal fiefdoms. Ideal for fans as long as it works, and they've proved that you can buy success.

Plus

The money provided by the individual
No need to account in any normal business sense

Minus

They could take their money and run
No need to consider anyone else's views

MODEL THREE
A public businesss

Tottenham, pre-Glazer Manchester United

Shares can be owned by anyone who chooses to buy, including fans. Large blocks of shares are in the hands of institutions and wealthy individuals – all of whom can sell for a price. The business has to be run transparently because it is open to public scrutiny by its shareholders.

Plus

Can generate needed capital

Run in interests of shareholders

Minus

Run in interests of shareholders

You could be taken over by a US soccer franchise

MODEL FOUR

Club class

Real Madrid, Barcelona

The club is made up of members who have voting rights, electing the president and managing committee on a regular basis.

Plus

Football comes before profit

Everyone owns an emotional stake

Minus

Can lead to management turmoil

Democracy can throw up disastrous presidents

MODEL FIVE
A family affair

Liverpool, Juventus

Ownership of the club is in the hands of a family trust and they take decisions on succession.

Plus
The club is generally run by people who care for tradition

Relative stability

Minus
Would you trust your family with your business?

Resistance to change when necessary

Competing for attention

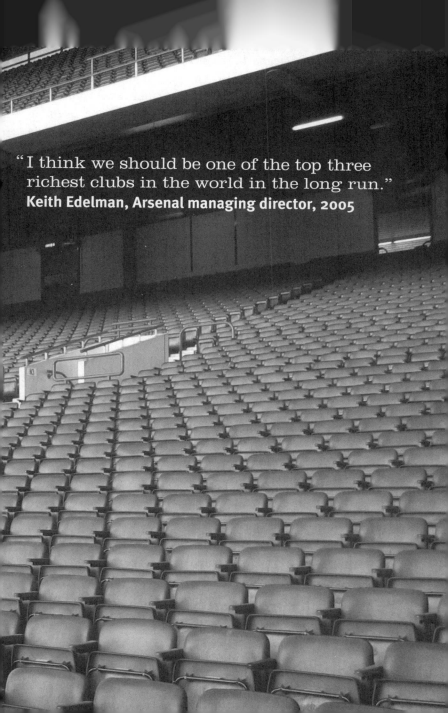

"I think we should be one of the top three richest clubs in the world in the long run."
Keith Edelman, Arsenal managing director, 2005

If you had asked any Arsenal fan twenty years ago to name the club's chief rivals, the name Tottenham Hotspur would almost certainly have topped the list. Other big English clubs would no doubt have received the odd mention, Manchester United and Liverpool of course, maybe Chelsea and West Ham, purely on the grounds of local pride. Anyone mentioning foreign clubs would have been regarded as eccentric at best, particularly considering Arsenal's underwhelming forays into Europe.

The same question asked now would no doubt generate a different response. Most fans now would list Chelsea and Manchester United as Arsenal's main rivals. Spurs would no doubt still appear on that list, but more through habit and proximity than anything else. Now, mention of foreign clubs as rivals to Arsenal wouldn't appear so strange, though Arsenal are still underperforming in Europe.

Of course, few Arsenal supporters would seriously consider Real Madrid or AC Milan as their main rivals. Rivalry is built up over time, and requires that teams play each other on a regular basis. The real roots of a rivalry can often be forgotten by all but the die-hard, as is the case with the rivalry between Arsenal and Spurs. What has changed though is the market that Arsenal, and all football clubs, are operating in. Football, just like any other business, is these days a globalised concern. This means that, in economic terms at least, Real Madrid and AC Milan really are among Arsenal's chief rivals. Increasingly Europe's superclubs are in competition with each other not only on the pitch, but in the race to exploit new markets, Asia and the United States in particular. As Time.com chief editor Tony Karon puts it:

"Scan news photographs from around the world, today, and you're as likely to see an Arsenal or Manchester United shirt at a Beijing college campus as at a demonstration of radical Shiites in Baghdad."

Posted on Time.com, 20th July 2004

In this context it is unsurprising that the clubs themselves have started to think, and talk, of themselves as brands. A look at Juventus's official website for example reveals that they have set themselves three objectives. The first, Juventus fans will be pleased to read, does relate to success on the pitch. The second objective refers directly to the development of the Juventus brand:

"Enhancement of its brand value with a view to consolidating and building the profile of Juventus Football Club S.p.A as a testimonial for the business world in order to further develop its commercial activities also by broadening its fan base in countries that have shown recent interest for the world of football."

Juventus.com

The language used may be somewhat indigestible but it is significant that Juventus's website is available in an English version in the first place. Indeed, Juventus's, and AC Milan's website can be viewed in Italian, English or Chinese. Arsenal have also realised the potential of the Asian market, posting content on Arsenal.com in Chinese.

Arsenal are not unique in this among English clubs of course. Manchester United also feature Chinese content on their website, and in many ways it is to Manchester United that other clubs have looked when it comes to developing their brand. This seems like a good place to start then in our look at Arsenal's rival brands, with the club who, over the last ten years, have consistently been Arsenal's greatest rival.

Manchester United

No other club has been quite as open, or successful, in aggressively developing its brand as Manchester United. It's the strength of the

Manchester United brand, plus the fact that alongside Real Madrid they are the world's best supported side, which made the club so attractive to new owner Malcolm Glazer. Glazer, an American tycoon and owner of the Tampa Bay Buccaneers (an American Football club), has made no pretence of being a United fan for anything but business reasons. He clearly sees United as an opportunity to make money, something which football clubs are notoriously bad at doing.

If any club can make Glazer money, though, it probably is Manchester United. According to the latest Deloitte and Touche analysis of football's richest clubs, in 2004 United had the largest turnover of any football club in the world (see p. 123). United turned over £171.5 million in this year – though to put this in perspective, this is similar to the amount just one branch of a medium-sized supermarket would turnover. In terms of brand recognition and loyalty football clubs may be giants, but in actual money-making terms they are little more than minnows.

Manchester United's fans demonstrate outside Old Trafford against the possible take over by Malcolm Glazer

This though is not what will have interested Glazer. He has invested his money (and a lot of debt) on future potential. David Haigh, Chief Executive of brand valuation consultancy Brand Finance, estimated that of the £800 million Glazer spent to acquire Manchester United, only £200 million was spent on actual tangible assets:

> "Therefore £600m is attributable to undisclosed intangible assets such as the brand, internally generated players and commercial contracts... We estimate the Manchester United brand is worth £225 million, making it a key asset in the takeover package."
>
> Quoted on accountancyage.com

Glazer is gambling a lot of money on being able to turn this intangible brand value into tangible, and significant, profit.

How though does he intend to do this? Ironically, despite the protests of many United fans that the club has sold its soul, he will probably change little about the way the club does business. United fans protesting about the large amount of debt that the club has taken on certainly have a point – those protesting solely on the basis that United have sold their identity as a football club are unfortunately about 15 years too late. Manchester United were already an extremely slick, commercially-focused business before Glazer took over. Indeed, this is partly what attracted him in the first place. In an interview with an online advertising industry website last year, Ben Hatton, then United's commercial development director had this to say:

> "We're a business first and foremost. And we're a complicated business. We're not just into the football business. We are also a:

1. Conferencing and catering business
2. Museum business – housing memorabilia
3. TV business – own global channel
4. Magazine business
5. Cinema business
6. Merchandise business
7. Seller of rights."

Quoted on biz.community.com

Ben Hatton left Manchester United shortly after the Glazer takeover, but his vision is certainly one that Glazer will wish to continue. United, before and after Glazer, operate with the intention to exploit the Manchester United brand to its full potential, and they do this to an extent that Arsenal are either unwilling, or unable to do.

The clearest indication of this can be seen in Arsenal and Manchester United's differing attitudes to overseas markets. When it comes down to their treatment of their fans (or customers as they might prefer) there is actually little difference in the way most Premiership clubs operate. Ticket prices will go up every year, a new replica shirt will be released, fans will not be consulted about the way the club is run, unconditional loyalty is taken as a given. The big attraction for Glazer is the money to be made overseas, and this is a road United were already some way down before his arrival.

It's not that Arsenal don't recognise the potential money to be made from the Asian and US markets. The presence of Chinese content on their website indicates that they clearly do. There are though two key differences between Arsenal and United which have led to this divergence of approach. Firstly, Arsenal just do not enjoy anything like the levels of support worldwide that United do. Arsenal's global fanbase is estimated at around 27 million people, making it one of the best supported clubs in the world. However, Manchester United have over 50 million supporters worldwide, with around 23 million in China alone. Suddenly the club's eagerness to take part in pre-season tours of China becomes understandable.

Of course, not all of these 'supporters' support the club in a way which most fans would recognise. Obviously the vast majority of United's 50 million supporters (or of Arsenal's 27 million) will never visit the ground. They probably have no family or local ties to the club. It might not ruin their weekend if the team loses. What they can do is consume. These millions of supporters can show their support for the club in the only way open to them, by buying replica shirts, subscribing to online TV services, by taking on a club-branded credit card. When clubs speak of having 50 million supporters worldwide, what they really mean is that they have 50 million consumers.

Thierry Henry signing autographs on the back of a fan during a promotional event for a sponsor at an event in Shenzhen, Southern China, Sunday, 3rd July, 2005

This brings us on to a second difference between Arsenal and Manchester United. Until recently, United were a publicly listed company, whose shares were available for anyone to buy on the stock market. Legally, any such company has to be run for the benefit of its shareholders. This of course gives them another, non-footballing reason, to wish to increase their turnover. Nor will this change under Glazer. Arsenal by contrast have always been privately owned by just a few, Arsenal supporting, individuals. Whatever you may think of the decisions the board makes, few Arsenal fans would contend that the decisions aren't taken with the best interests of the club at heart, and for ultimately footballing reasons. Arsenal, of course, want to make more money, but purely to improve their chances of success on the pitch. This represents an important point of difference between the two clubs. United, focused on expanding their business interests overseas spend every pre-season dragging an exhausted set of players through a series of meaningless friendlies in the USA and Asia. Arsenal by contrast generally engage in some low-key friendlies against Austrian part-timers and Barnet. There is no financial gain in this, but it is what the manager wants to get the best out of his players. Alex Ferguson, the United manager, has at times been openly critical of his club's pre-season routine, but is powerless to change it. Arsenal, for all that the club takes an increasingly commercial view of things, is still a football brand first, and a business second. Unfortunately for United fans, the reverse has been true at their club for some time.

Chelsea

An unexpected challenge to Manchester United's position as England's leading football brand has arisen since 2003. While Arsenal have pretty much matched United on the pitch in recent years, they could never compete with them off it. With the arrival of Roman Abramovich in English football, United cannot take their off-field dominance for granted anymore. If anyone at Manchester United was slow to realise this, the point would surely have been hammered home to them when their chief executive, Peter Kenyon, suddenly left United in September 2003 to take up the same position at Abramovich's Chelsea. Kenyon, a self-professed United fan doubled his salary upon moving to Stamford Bridge; from this snapshot alone it is clear where Kenyon's priorities seem to lie.

Manchester United were already the dominant financial force in English football when Kenyon joined them in 1997 as deputy chief executive. Having joined United from Umbro, he soon signalled his ruthlessness by cancelling United's shirt contract with Umbro, and signing up instead with Nike. Having succeeded Martin Edwards as chief executive in 2000, it was Kenyon who oversaw United's push for overseas growth, and this no doubt appealed to Abramovich when he was looking for someone to run his new club. Abramovich is reported to have fallen in love with football at a Manchester United–Real Madrid game at Old Trafford. The recruitment of Kenyon suggests that Abramovich liked what he saw off the pitch, just as much as on.

Chelsea, much like Manchester United, have been a highly-commercialised business for some years. In an article published in 2002, pre-Abramovich, Dan Bobby a consultant at brand specialists Wolff Olins had this to say about the Chelsea and Arsenal brands:

"Chelsea is a business which includes a football club. It is listed on the stock market as Chelsea Village plc and counts football as 'one of its activities' while Arsenal is a football club first and a business second."

Guardian, 4th May 2002

It was the vision of former chairman Ken Bates that football would be just one of Chelsea's core activities, with their diversification into leisure and hospitality activities bringing in more money than football alone ever could. Of course it didn't quite work out this way, and Chelsea Village plc, the name Bates gave the publicly listed company Chelsea had become, were £80 million in debt when

Abramovich took over. Chelsea's attempts at diversification having largely failed, they changed their name to Chelsea Football Club plc in 2005, a symbolic attempt to re-brand Chelsea as, once again, a football club first, and a business second.

Naturally, this re-focusing on football as their core business doesn't mean that Chelsea have neglected the development of their brand off the pitch. This is the job Kenyon was brought in to do, and in the summer of 2005, in between goading Arsenal and United, Kenyon claimed that it was his aim to turn Chelsea into a normal, self-sufficient business within five years. His strategy to achieve this is simple, to replicate the work he carried out at United, and turn Chelsea into a global brand.

Chelsea do not have the kind of worldwide support that United, or Arsenal, enjoy. This simple fact will lead to a couple of important changes of emphasis when it comes to managing their brand. While at United, Kenyon argued strongly for the unbundling of overseas TV rights, an action which would have seen United enriched at the expense of the rest of the Premiership. Interestingly Kenyon now argues that collective bargaining on TV deals must stay. Simple altruism? This is unlikely. Simply put, Chelsea do not yet have the kind of global pulling power to gain from the unbundling of TV rights. As things stand they know they are better off with the status quo. Instead Chelsea intend to focus more on new technologies, such as broadband and mobile phones. Chris Tait, managing director of Chelsea Digital Media had this to say in August 2005:

"Among the core age group of 13–25-year-olds, there is much more demand for mobile content than TV services. They want to see clips of goals, not live matches."

Quoted on brandrepublic.com, 3rd August 2005

This also provides another reason, apart from the reported £8 million a year involved, for Chelsea's new sponsorship deal with Samsung, an electronics manufacturer. It should not be forgotten that Kenyon tied up a similar deal with Vodafone while he was chief executive at Manchester United.

A look at Chelsea's website is instructive; as yet they have not provided Chinese content, as Arsenal and Manchester United have done. They do, though, provide a Chelsea-branded broadband service, and Chelsea TV, currently available to 27 million homes in 17 countries. This service still lags behind United's MUTV, which is available to 80 million homes in 68 countries. But Chelsea are catching up.

Bruce Buck, Chairman of Chelsea, has identified four key regions in which Chelsea would like to improve their profile: Russia, China, the United States, and London. Buck's choice of London as an area they need to improve their profile is interesting, and hints at the distance Chelsea still need to travel to become a global brand. Currently they are not even the best supported club in London, let alone the world. Continued success on the pitch will inevitably bring a greater profile, more prestige, more support. As long as Chelsea do that it is easy to envisage that in two or three years time they could be the world's richest club, and one of its most recognisable brands. In some ways the chief danger to Chelsea lies within. The abrasiveness of Kenyon has done little to endear Chelsea to fans of other clubs, or neutral supporters. This in turn makes them less attractive to sponsors. Another danger is that if Chelsea dominate too much, the league becomes uncompetitive, thus damaging the brand of football itself. Some fear this is already happening. Malcolm Clarke, chairman of the Football Supporters Association had this to say about Chelsea's failure to sell-out a home game at the start of the 2005–06 season:

"When Peter Kenyon says it's a one-horse race, he should realise that what follows is hardly surprising. How many racehorse punters want to go and watch a one-horse race. Maybe Mr Kenyon should be asked why fans should pay £48 to watch a one-horse race?"

Quoted in the *Independent* newspaper, 26th August 2005

This is something worth remembering for those who see football as just another business. There are a thousand differences between football and any other business, most centring on football's sheer irrationality and unpredictability. In football, too much success can be as much of a turn-off as too little.

Tottenham Hotspur

For much of Chelsea's history they were not only overshadowed by Arsenal, but also by Arsenal's North London rivals, Spurs. Now, though Spurs are showing signs of recovery on the pitch, there is no doubt that they lie a distant third in London's pecking order. Spurs, as any Arsenal fan will happily tell you, haven't won the League since 1961. Nor have they won the FA Cup since 1991, or a European trophy since 1984. Their only success in recent years has been the now-devalued League Cup, delivered to them by ex-Arsenal manager George Graham, in 1999. Nor have things been much better off the pitch for Spurs. Their position in the 2004 Deloitte and Touche rich list was 14th, their turnover of £66 million barely half that of Arsenal.

Things weren't always this way. As we mentioned in the first chapter, as recently as the 1980s Spurs were as big a club as Arsenal, and at the time more glamorous and successful. Spurs downfall was in large part brought about by their attempts to do what Manchester United did so successfully ten years later – capitalise on their brand and diversify their business.

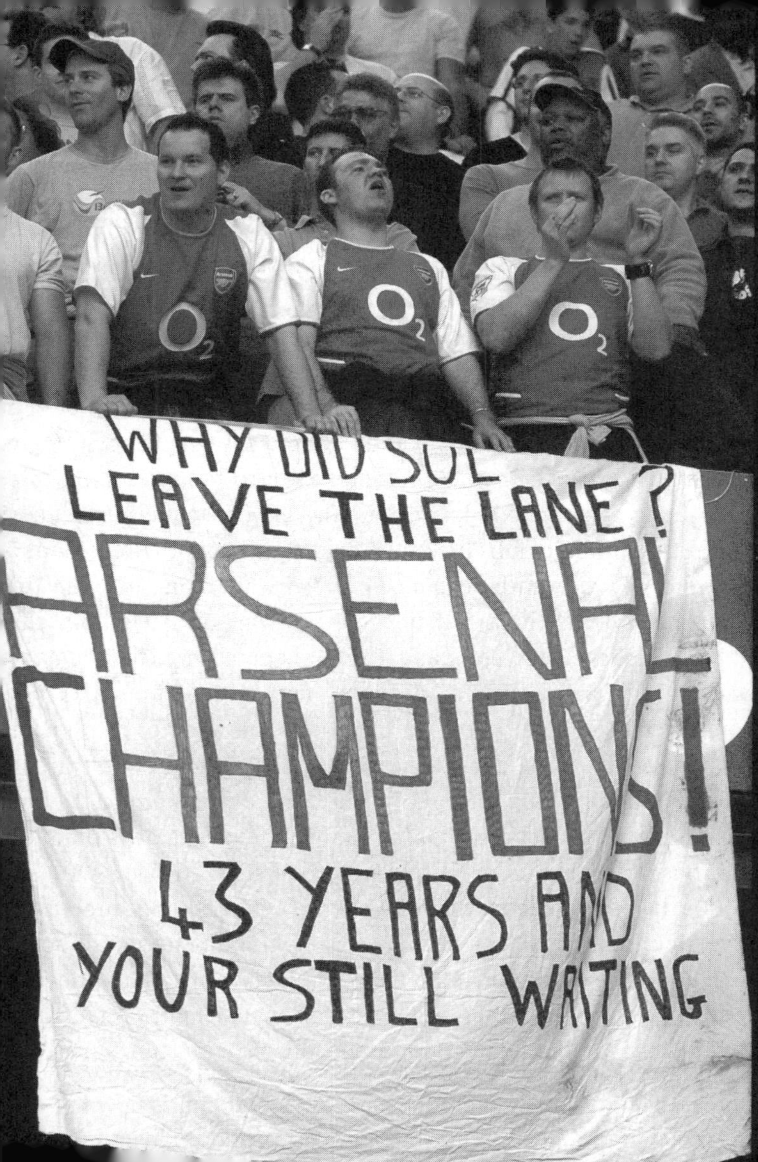
WHY DID SOL
LEAVE THE LANE ?
ARSENAL
CHAMPIONS!
43 YEARS AND
YOUR STILL WAITING

Spurs began this process in the early eighties. While re-developing their ground Spurs incorporated 72 executive boxes into the stadium. This was an enormous number for the time, and sure enough, Spurs could not sell them all. If anything, Spurs were merely ahead of their time. Post Italia 90 their boxes would have made money. As it was, in the still hooligan-blighted 1980s, they lost the club money. They also lost the club goodwill, with many of Spurs' most diehard supporters being displaced from their regular terrace position on 'The Shelf' as part of the re-development.

Spurs were also the first club to float on the stock exchange. Traditionally English clubs were protected from asset-stripping chairmen by FA rule 34, which placed strict limits on the amount of dividends that clubs could pay their directors. Irving Scholar, Spurs chairman from November 1982, found a way to circumvent this rule; by creating a separate holding company, which would in effect own Spurs the football club, he could float the holding company as a plc, and pay dividends to himself and his directors. In 1984 this was exactly what Scholar did, becoming the first British football club to be a publicly listed company. From this point on Scholar's name became synonymous with the worst excesses of football's new commercialised face. To be fair to Scholar, he was not responsible for the executive box debacle, having actually bought into the club after this affair brought Spurs to the brink of bankruptcy. Neither were many of his actions that far removed from business practices that became common practice for football clubs in the 1990s and 2000s. In his wrangles with the FA over TV deals, and his attempts to diversify Spurs' business portfolio through an ill-fated partnership with Sportswear company Hummel, Scholar laid out a blueprint that Martin Edwards and then Peter Kenyon would follow years later. Except that, unlike Edwards and Kenyon, Scholar and Spurs only lost money.

Spurs have recovered from the effects of the Scholar era only in very recent years. Alan Sugar tried and failed to make sense of football's 'prune-juice' economics for a number of years, but his unwillingness to spend vast sums of money on new players never endeared him to the fans. Spurs are now owned by a private company, ENIC, and under the chairmanship of Daniel Levy they seem somewhat more stable again. It helps of course that, finally, they seem to be improving on the pitch, but they also seem to be making efforts to move their brand forward again. In April 2005 Spurs appointed Paul Barber, formerly European chief executive of Ogilvy PR, to head up Spurs' commercial and marketing efforts, and the exploitation of the Spurs brand in the UK and overseas. The role is similar to Peter Kenyon's at Chelsea, though without the addition of player negotiations. When every big club throughout Europe is looking to exploit its brand to the full, Spurs would be foolish not to try and improve their efforts in this area. In doing this though they need to bear in mind the lessons of their own history, which graphically illustrate the dangers of over-reaching yourself, and of forgetting why the club, the players and the fans are there in the first place. If they need reminding, they should refer to the words Spurs manager Keith Burkinshaw is reported to have disgustedly muttered as he walked out on Tottenham, having fallen out with Irving Scholar in 1984: "There used to be a football club over there."

Celtic and Rangers

Barring the odd pre-season or testimonial game Arsenal's direct contact with the Glasgow giants has been limited. Given the choice, Celtic and Rangers would prefer to find themselves in direct opposition to Arsenal at least twice a season, playing in the English Premier League. Looked at in purely financial terms it is easy to see why this move would appeal. Celtic and Rangers both command a massive fanbase, each averaging over 50,000 supporters for home matches. In addition they both have millions of fans around the world, particularly in Ireland, and that much-coveted territory, the USA.

Despite this support, both clubs are massively in debt. As of late 2005, Celtic were £20 million in debt, while Rangers had debts of more than three times that figure. A move to play in the English Premier League would not only wipe out much of this debt at a stroke, but would also enable both clubs to develop their brand much further than they will ever be able to in Scotland. The English Premier League is the most-watched domestic league in the world,

Rangers fans from abroad

the Scottish Premier League attracts little interest outside Scotland, and is increasingly uncompetitive. It is hard to ever see this changing – Scotland has a population of just over 5 million people, less than London, and this alone means that the Scottish Premier League will never be able to compete with Europe's bigger leagues.

However, there are a number of good reasons why it is unlikely to happen. Neither UEFA nor FIFA are keen, believing that such a move would erode national boundaries, and could pave the way for an eventual European superleague. They have rejected calls for a 'Northern Europe' league, made up of the biggest clubs from

Scotland, Holland and Scandanavia, for similar reasons. Smaller English Premier League clubs are never likely to vote for such a move either, as it would result in two fewer spaces being available in the Premier League for them. Another potential stumbling block is that currently each of the home nations has a separate FA and national team. If Scottish teams started to play in England it would certainly weaken the case to continue with four separate national associations.

One could also argue that to a large extent, Celtic and Rangers problems are of their own making. At their instigation, the rules were changed in the eighties allowing home clubs to keep all of their gate receipts, whereas previously they were split with the visiting club. A similar move occurred in England, but its effects were less obvious, due to the greater number of well-supported clubs south of the border. The cumulative attendance of the other ten clubs in the Scottish Premier League is less than that of Celtic and Rangers alone, resulting in a vast financial imbalance. This has led to a fall in playing standards, which in turn has driven attendances down still lower. The chances of any club outside the big two challenging for the title in Scotland are minimal, but the lack of competition means that both Celtic and Rangers are not best prepared to compete in Europe, often resulting in early exits and a further loss of revenue.

Celtic and Rangers are another fine example of how too much success in too few hands can damage the overall football brand. Neither have they made the most of what they do have. The main difference financially between the Glasgow giants and their English counterparts is the size of their TV deals. Obviously the Scottish league cannot command anywhere near the money the English Premier League does, and it is this that is responsible for the financial gap between England and Scotland. Nonetheless both Glasgow giants have massive attendances and merchandising operations, enough to put both of them into the top 20 of football's 2004 rich list. Rangers just made it in at number 19, while Celtic managed a respectable 13th place, above Spurs. Their levels of turnover should be enough to allow each club to maintain a competitive squad and stay out of debt. Football clubs do not provide many examples of well run businesses though, and Celtic and Rangers are not among the few. This quote from David Murray, Rangers majority shareholder and honorary chairman is illustrative of a common problem in football's board rooms:

> "They always say that football chairmen and businessmen are sensible but they leave their brains outside the ground when they go into the stadium. I think you do get affected by supporter pressure, your own pressure, the chase for success."

The Scotsman, 5th May 2005

Juventus and AC Milan

In Italy football chairmen are affected by the "chase for success" mentioned by David Murray to a greater extent than anywhere else. The most passionate supporters, the Ultras, demand success and have been known to pay visits to the club's training grounds to register their displeasure verbally and physically. Both the Milan and the Rome derbies had to be abandoned after crowd trouble in 2005, and the overall atmosphere of intimidation and violence is certainly comparable with anything that occurred in England during the 70s and 80s. In addition, Italian clubs are beset by accusations of financial irregularities and match-fixing. In 2005 Genoa gained promotion back to Serie A, only to be demoted again before the start of the 2005-06 season, having been found guilty of match-fixing.

It is against this backdrop that the Italian giants, Juventus (of Turin) and AC Milan operate. As well as being the two best supported and historically successful clubs in Italy, both Juventus and AC Milan are owned by multi-billionaires, giving them the advantage of stability at the top, and increased transfer funds. Not that this advantage has helped the third of Italy's biggest clubs, Internazionale of Milan. Inter owner, Massimo Moratti has spent hundreds of millions of pounds since the beginning of the 90s, with little return for his investment. Juventus have been owned by the Agnelli family (also owners of Fiat) since 1923, while AC Milan has been owned since 1986 by Italian prime minister Silvio Berlusconi. The conflict of interest inherent in the Italian prime minister also owning one of the country's biggest football teams, is further complicated by the fact that Berlusconi also owns many of Italy's national TV channels. Unsurprisingly, AC Milan TV, launched in 1999, is a success.

Though the same controversy does not surround the ownership of Juventus, the club has been hit by scandal of its own. In late 2004 the club doctor, Riccardo Agricola, was convicted under sporting fraud laws of doping offences alleged to have taken place during the mid-90s. This has led to calls for Juventus to be stripped of the trophies they won during that period, though unfortunately Juventus were unlikely to be alone in breaking the rules.

None of this scandal has done much to dent either club's popularity at home or abroad. Juventus are still Italy's best-supported club, though much like Manchester United, they tend to draw most of their support from the wider country, rather than their home city. Unlike Manchester United's army of fans, few Juventus fans make the journey to see their team in the flesh; between 1998 and 2004 Juventus enjoyed only the fifth largest average attendances in Italy with 39,445. Inter had the highest average attendance with 58,743, while AC Milan were just behind with 55,523. This goes some way to explaining the ground development work Juventus are currently engaged in. For at the same time that Arsenal are building a new ground in order to increase their stadium capacity from 38,000 to 60,000, Juventus are re-developing their existing ground to reduce capacity from 70,000 to 35,000. The Stadio Delle Alpi was only built in 1990, for the World Cup finals, but it has proved unpopular with the fans. The planned changes will bring the stands much closer to the pitch, improving the atmosphere, and will also incorporate executive boxes, helping to make up the money lost in ticket sales. Juventus, in common with Arsenal, also plan to sell naming rights to the stadium, the first Italian club to do so.

Possibly the most significant aspect of Juventus's re-development plans though is that they have also invested more than £20 million in leasing their ground from the council. This means that, as for the vast majority of English clubs, all of the income generated by the stadium will go to Juventus. This is not commonly the case in Italy, or elsewhere on the continent, where the local council often owns the stadium. The San Siro for example, home to both Milan clubs, is owned by the council, massively reducing their matchday revenues. This goes someway to explaining why AC Milan and Juventus aren't challenging Manchester United for the title of the world's richest club; AC Milan lay third in the 2004 rich list, with a turnover of £147 million, while Juventus lay fifth with £142 million. This is emphasised in Deloitte and Touche's annual review of football finance for 2005:

"Matchday revenues grew in each of the five leagues analysed, except Italy... Absolute performance in this area varies greatly with the English premiership total of 588 euros in 2003/04, higher than the matchday revenues of all the French Ligue 1, German Bundesliga and Italian Serie A clubs combined."

Deloitte and Touche, *Annual Review of Football Finance*,
Highlights, p. 1

Juventus obviously see this as a key area to improve in; an option that isn't currently open to AC Milan. Where both clubs are focusing, in common with many of Europe's other big clubs, is on the overseas markets. In recent years Juventus have played pre-season tours in Japan and the United States, and have opened a Juventus store in

Tokyo. AC Milan have also toured the United States and Asia, while their slick website boasts content in an impressive five languages; Italian, English, Portugese, Japanese and Chinese. The presence of Portugese content points the way to a possible future market for Europe's superclubs – Brazil, and the rest of South America.

Barcelona and Real Madrid

Spain's system of club ownership is utterly unlike anything to be found in the other big European leagues, where generally dictatorial chairmen rule the roost. This isn't to say that the men who run the big Spanish clubs aren't as egotistical as their counterparts in Italy or England; they are however elected by their clubs' members. Joan Laporta was elected Barcelona president in 2003, on the back of a promise to attempt to sign David Beckham. The Beckham deal never happened, of course, for he instead went to play his part in Florentino Perez's 'Galacticos' strategy at Real Madrid. Perez was elected Real Madrid president in 2000, having promised to sign Luis Figo from, of all clubs, Barcelona. Incredibly Perez delivered, and a key part of his brand strategy has been to sign one Galactico a season ever since, using them as a spearhead to push on into previously unconquered territory.

For Barcelona the failure to sign Beckham undoubtedly cost them money, such is the appeal of Brand Beckham around the world. It may have proved a blessing in disguise though, for the player they signed instead, Ronaldinho, is now widely acknowledged to be one of the finest players in the world, and helped Barca to the Spanish title in 2005. Real Madrid were also interested in Ronaldinho, before eventually signing Beckham instead. A quote attributed to an un-named Real official gave this reason why:

"Between Ronaldinho and Beckham, I'd go for Beckham a hundred times. Just look how

FC Barcelona's player Ronaldinho, duels for the ball against Real Madrid's David Beckham, during their League soccer match in Madrid, Sunday, 10th April 2005

handsome Beckham is, the class he has, the image. The whole of Asia has fallen in love with us because of Beckham. Ronaldinho is too ugly."

Quoted on Guardian.co.uk, 26th April 2004

This unattributed quote seems almost too good to be true; whether true or not, it is certainly believable, and does contain an essential truth about Real Madrid's recruitment policies. Since 2000, Real have recruited players as much for what they can bring to the brand of Real Madrid as the team.

Perez's strategy has certainly succeeded off the pitch. Real's revenue almost doubled in the three years between 2001 and 2004, meaning that by 2004 they stood second only to Manchester United in football's rich list, with a turnover of £156 million. At times the strategy has also worked on the pitch, as world-class players such as Zidane, Carlos and Figo delivered Spanish titles in 2001 and 2003, and the Champions League in 2002. Real have won nothing since, though given the sheer quality of players they can afford to recruit, they will always be competitive. There have also been complaints from both within and outside Real Madrid that the club has become too commercialised. This quote from Emil Butragueno, Real's vice-president makes clear Real's current priorities:

"It is not only what the clubs take at the gate, one has to look further afield. It is a case of creating and exploiting a new market, generating illusions, attracting thousands of fans, making lasting impressions, achieving long-term income by making the brand name known."

Quoted on india4u.com, 17th August 2005

This blatant prioritising of marketing over football considerations has drawn criticism from, among others, Fernando Hierro, former Real captain and icon. In an interview explaining his reasons for leaving Real Madrid he had this to say:

> **"We had different views on how the game should be run...Football's about kicking a ball on a field. Nothing else. Too much marketing and merchandising can take your eye off the ball."**
>
> Quoted in *Guardian*, 16th September 2004

The criticism of Real Madrid has come from outside the club as well. Those on the receiving end of Real Madrid's aggressive approach to player acquisitions (Arsenal among them in the case of Anelka and Vieira) have had frequent cause to complain about Real's high-handed approach. Santos president Marcelo Teixeira, attempting to resist Real's wooing of Brazil's latest prodigy, Robinho, had this to say in the summer of 2005:

> **"It's a lack of respect for Santos...They might have economic and financial power but it doesn't mean that they can do what they want, when they want."**
>
> Quoted on bbc.co.uk, 21st July 2005

Teixeira was wrong about this. Real can do pretty much what they want, when they want. Robinho inevitably became Real's 'Galactico' signing for 2005, despite the attempts of Arsène Wenger to sign him for Arsenal.

Not even Barcelona, a massive club themselves, can compete with the strength of Real Madrid's brand image and financial muscle, as Real's signing of Luis Figo from them in 2000 showed.

Barcelona have always studiously cultivated a different kind of image from that projected by Real, one that at times has been consciously constructed in direct opposition to Real. Historically Real were Spain's establishment club, not only because of their obvious association with the Spanish capital, but also because they were Franco's favourite club. Indeed, it wasn't unknown for Franco to directly interfere in player transfers, as he did in the case of Alfredo di Stefano, ensuring that di Stefano signed for Real rather than Barca. Barcelona by contrast were seen as a symbol of Catalonian nationalism, and were often the only legitimate outlet for Catalonians whose culture and language were suppressed by Franco.

These differences have had a direct influence on the kinds of brands that Real and Barca have built. Real, as under Franco, can still buy whoever they want, and have made this ability a central part of their brand strategy. Unfortunately, the less palatable associations with Franco, most obviously his fascistic ideals, are also still associated with the club, mainly through Real's right-wing ultras. Barcelona still position themselves as Catalonia's national team, and despite their own size and popularity, are still seen as being a more anti-establishment club, at least in comparison with Real. As the 2005–06 season kicked off Barcelona did not, and have never had, any kind of sponsor's logo on the front of their shirt. This decision, a vital part of any club's brand strategy, had always been taken in order to preserve the integrity of the Barcelona shirt. For Barca fans, who view the Barca shirt as representative of all Catalonia, it would have been akin to putting a sponsor's name on the front of the England shirt. In 2004 this changed. Barcelona members were asked to vote on whether to allow shirt sponsorship (members' approval was required before the club could make any changes), and the response was an overwhelming yes. That Barcelona had no shirt sponsor in 2005 was no longer due to principle, but merely to the fact that no one had yet offered Barca enough money. Viewing themselves as every bit the equal of Real or Manchester United,

Barca have held out for at least the £12 million a year that those two clubs receive from their sponsors. Once someone offers enough, one of the last un-branded spaces in world football will disappear.

This demonstrates one of the effects of football's drive towards commercialisation; those key differences between different clubs, different brands, disappear. Once every club operates in the same way, what is there to differentiate one club from its rival? That Barcelona are now every bit as marketing-driven as Real, United, AC Milan or Chelsea is apparent from its activities during the summer of 2005. Barca, like most of the European elite, flew off to overseas markets for a lucrative tour, in this case, to Asia. Finishing off the tour in Macao, Barca romped to an easy win, but manager Frank Rijkaard complained about the state of the pitch, Barcelona goalkeeper Ruben Martinez was admitted to hospital with heatstroke, while ex-Arsenal midfielder Giovanni van Bronckhorst simply had this to say:

"These trips are not good."

Quoted on india4u.com, 17th August 2005

The point is further hammered home at Barca's online store; it's a very glossy and professional site, but it appears to be as much about Barca's kit manufacturer, Nike, as it is about Barca. The site sells not only Barca kit, but also that of other clubs with Nike manufactured kit, Arsenal and Manchester United among them.

There is an important lesson here for any club; focus on the marketing above the football, and you risk losing everything which made your brand valuable and unique in the first place.

Chapter 7

The future's bright, is it red and white?

You weren't world-class when Arsenal signed you."
Arsène Wenger's reported response to Patrick Vieira's complaint that Arsenal had failed to sign world-class players

What does the future hold for Arsenal? The club and everyone involved with it stand expectant, a little apprehensive, hoping for the best while, deep down, fearing the worst. Feeling pretty much like any fan as you wait for the whistle to blow. But this time, when the whistle blows, it will signal the end of Arsenal's time at Highbury Stadium and usher in a new era at Ashburton Grove. The move is small in geographical terms, a mere half mile down the road, but of potentially enormous significance in just about every other way.

Arsenal need have no financial concerns, according to its managing director, Keith Edelman. Speaking at the start of the 2005–06 season, Edelman confidently predicted that the new stadium would add £30 million to profits each year – making Arsenal, in prospect at least, the most profitable club in the UK. But everything depends on performances on the pitch. Having built a stadium fit for one of the world's great teams, will Arsenal be able to deliver? And, as always in football, there are no guarantees on that. The greatest reason for optimism about the future comes from the continued guidance of Arsène Wenger. In ten years he has created a legend for himself that no one in Arsenal's history, not even Herbert Chapman, can match. "Arsène knows" and "Trust Arsène" are the words spoken by the fans. Business analyst Professor Tom Cannon described him as "probably the biggest asset in European football". But who follows after Arsène?

The greatest reassurance is that Arsène Wenger has become a legend because of his ability to think ahead of everybody else. There is a feeling that he could put up the team sheet for the opening game of a season three years in advance – and it would include unexpected as well as unknown names, and one or two planned absentees. (The reality of this was shown when, in January 2006 as this book went to print, Arsenal signed Diaby, Adebayor and Walcott.) And he's probably already planned his own succession. As a representative of the Arsenal brand, Arsène Wenger has added layers of sophistication, style and wisdom that it did not possess before his arrival. The main criticisms of his approach from those who have passed through Arsenal have come from discarded English players. While fans might sometimes regret the loss of Merson, Upson, Pennant and Bentley, the objective assessment is that none of them have been 'world-class'. Arsène and Arsenal now seek world-class performance on the pitch. Although it sometimes seems harsh to talented English players, Arsenal's judgements are made against the highest criteria. This in itself, rather than a more sentimentally nationalistic approach to team-building, is the best guarantee of continuing success.

The competition on the pitch will not weaken. A Big Four in the Premiership seems likely for the foreseeable future: Arsenal, Chelsea, Manchester United and Liverpool. Chelsea's footballing foundations will become stronger as the years go by, even as the money spent on players declines and as the need to spend diminishes. By 2010 their objective is to be operating like a normal club, not dependent on the wealth of an individual. By then, real assets will have been accumulated anyway, leaving them equipped to cope without the massive cash injections of recent years.

Manchester United simply have to succeed or Malcolm Glazer will sell up and retreat to Florida. Our expectation is that he is a good enough businessman to leave knowledgeable people in charge of the team. Perhaps to the distress of the really hardcore Manchester United fans, Glazer will remain because he will make the money he needs to make. But more than any of the other clubs, Manchester United will be desperate for trophies to justify the status they perceive in their own eyes. But at some point soon the issue of managerial succession will need to be faced, since Sir Alex Ferguson cannot go on forever. Who replaces him will be a crucial decision.

We have included Liverpool in the Big Four, although their Premiership track record makes them very much fourth choice. Winning the European Champions Cup in 2005 showed that they are still a big club, although much reduced from their heydays in the 1980s. The depth of support, not just in Liverpool but around the world, remains. Other teams have the potential to rise again and compete against the Big Four. What is needed is a combination of resources, tradition and a loyal fan base that can be reenergised by success on the pitch. Newcastle, Everton, Aston Villa and Spurs are in this category.

Such a resurgence of competition should be welcomed by Arsenal even as they take steps to counter it as fiercely as possible on the football field. Nothing would actually threaten the Arsenal brand, and the whole commercial enterprise including the new stadium, as much as a weakening of competitiveness in the Premiership. The 'Scottish situation', whereby only two clubs ever have a realistic hope of success, would be disastrous for the Premiership. Indeed some have said that this is happening, and they point (often wrongly) to falling attendances. The fact is that the future success of the Arsenal brand depends on the continuing success of the overarching brand that is football itself. Football is the core product that any football brand feeds off, and the football institutions need to nurture the core product at all levels. Football needs to keep its ability to thrill, entertain and inspire dreams. Lack of competitiveness in the English league would threaten football's ability to do those things.

This became a burning issue at the beginning of the 2005–6 season. With Chelsea starting the new season unbeaten, the argument started to rage about the Premiership becoming boring. Chelsea, in particular, were accused of a boring style of football – "only winning matters, we don't care how". Unable to fill their relatively small stadium, it seemed that fans were telling them that the style mattered as well as the result. Jose Mourinho, the Chelsea manager, was interviewed about this but claimed not to have the words "boring" or "obligation" in his vocabulary. For how long could he do this if the crowds continued to drop, even if his team kept recording wins by not conceding a goal? Would people pay to see negative football? At the same time Arsène Wenger was reasserting his belief that football does have obligations to entertain the public. Two brands, two beliefs. The two beliefs are defined not just by different styles of play but different attitudes to responsibility.

A natural reflection of competitiveness is the cycle of success. Great teams come to a peak and then decline, before rebuilding and regeneration take them back up again. Failure is a necessary part of football and of life. It's a hard lesson that every football fan learns to appreciate from an early age. Chelsea are currently a threat to that natural cycle because their unnatural wealth enables them to avoid the risk of failure. In the normal cycle of success and failure, winning and losing, inevitable troughs occur while a manager waits for new players (homegrown or bought) to mature and settle into the team. Arsenal, in 2005–06, are in one of those troughs while Arsène Wenger builds what could be the third great team of his managership (1998, 2002–04, 2008?). The current team is young and inexperienced, but its footballing potential is richer than ever. If success comes with this team, Arsenal fans will take greater delight in having achieved it through sticking to fundamental principles. Football itself will be stronger for it, and it will give hope to all those who believe that success should be built not bought.

The answer for football is not to tinker with the core product. There was an advert by Budweiser, one of English football's sponsors, that played to the deepest fears of English football fans by announcing with much American razzamatazz a number of innovations. The renaming of a team as the 'Red and White Sox' and the introduction of 'the multi-ball shoot-out' made football fans smile – it was an uneasy smile (particularly among Manchester United supporters) because it seemed to have an element of truth. The fact is that there is always a lobby for change, whether of individual rules or competition structures, because sport thrives on debate. But only the most desperate of failing sports needs to make fundamental changes. Football is not in that situation. A breakaway to form a European league by the G-14 group, for example, would be a desperate move – and a self-destructive move.

The core product of football is in good shape and it will support the growth of individual football brands worldwide. But those brands need to see football's potential to do more than simply earn money.

Responsibility for developing football itself rests with national associations such as the FA (increasingly undermined by the more commercial objectives of the Premier League) and international associations such as UEFA and FIFA. Most football fans would place little faith in these institutions but they are in existence and, if you look at them objectively, best equipped to do the job of developing football. The fear would be that alternatives to replace them would be wholly controlled by the richest and most powerful.

This makes it even more imperative for football brands to use their power for altruistic as well as commercial reasons. Football will have no future if it is not nurtured at school, junior and grass roots levels. Football brands have the power to support the game at these levels and to play a broader social and educational role as well.

One of the interesting but barely publicised examples associated with Arsenal was the club's support of the London Urban Collective, a group of 30 young people in the Highbury area. The group was selected from 120 musical hopefuls who came to an audition. Once the group was chosen they were given life skills and music business training, leading to the release of a rap album in 2005. Arsenal's involvement was very low-key, at first not disclosed to many of the participants, but the project would not have happened without funding by the club. It was one of a number of initiatives taken to ensure that the move to a new stadium has a positive regenerative effect on the area.

The stadium's positive influence is a factor that is of particular interest to John Sorrell, a lifelong Arsenal fan who has been watching Arsenal for 53 years. Formerly Chairman of the Design Council and now Chairman of CABE (the Commission for Architecture and the Built Environment) John is equally passionate about using football and architecture for the public good. "What matters to me is not the features of the new stadium building itself but its impact on people – the way they see it, use it, play in it. On those terms the new Arsenal stadium can be a very significant building. But I'm sure it will also succeed on aesthetic and financial grounds too."

**ACQUIRED
FOR
ARSENAL F.C.
DEVELOPMENT**

A thony

020-7935 835

7 MANCHESTER SQUARE, LONDON W1M 5RE
www.anthonygreenandspencer.com

While saying that the sheer quality of the football is now higher and more pleasurable than at any other time in his life, John Sorrell sees the stadium as a key to Arsenal's future. "I'm interested in communities having icons – sometimes large but often small. A local library or a park can be an icon – they become part of people's lives, they feel ownership. You can't achieve this with a national stadium but you can with a local one. That's why it was so important that Arsenal didn't need to move far from Highbury. People underestimate the importance of the place. Much as we love the old stadium, if you want to play at the top level you have to have the quality to fit. Arsenal will manage it, and the stadium will be a treasured local icon."

The stadium is designed by HOK Sport but alongside it is another development by architects CZWG which covers almost as great an area. This adjacent site is given over to housing and community facilities, so that Arsenal's stadium will remain seamlessly housed within the residential neighbourhood. Over the coming years Highbury itself will be converted into flats to be designed by Allies and Morrison. Probably only the most wealthy of Arsenal's fans will be able even to contemplate buying a flat in the redeveloped Highbury. It has been a feature of Arsenal's (and London's) transformation over the last two decades that the socio-demographic make-up of the population has changed. To the regret of many fans, Arsenal's customer base has shifted upmarket, and the stadium has been gentrified.

The change has, of course, been brought about largely as a result of ticket pricing policies. Even one of the cheaper season ticket seats at Highbury costs £1,000, a price that is beyond the means of many ordinary fans, particularly if you want to go as a family. Arsenal has been raising its prices steeply, year by year over the last decade, anticipating the move to a new stadium. The move towards high prices has happened at a time of success on the pitch and a high standard of football. No doubt these factors have helped to stifle major protests, and Arsenal have become adept at giving 'members' little extras that have sweetened the pill of high prices. The commemorative package "Highbury: The Final Salute" – an enamel box containing gifts such as books (including Nick Hornby's *Fever Pitch* with a new two-page preface), a DVD, collection of images – is an impressive production. It was given free to Gold members. But to become a Gold member you had first to pay £1,000 plus to renew your season ticket.

However, there are stirrings of customer service in this approach, a development long overdue. Until very recently, in common with other British football teams, Arsenal have not had to consider customer service. But the need to fill a larger stadium has changed things, as has the demographic change in the customer base we mentioned before. Ben Evans, for example, is a fairly typical Arsenal fan. His family moved to Stoke Newington in 1968 and as a young boy Ben could hear the roar of the match day crowd from his garden. This mixture of location, his father's allegiance and school friends made him a natural Arsenal fan. By the age of 13 he was going regularly

R TIER SEATING

ONLY   MATCH No.

to matches, including away games. The love affair has continued, with many of his friends following a similar path. Now with young children of his own, the wheel rolls around again.

"There's a sense of legacy, a pleasure from taking new people and passing it on," Ben explained. "I'm now part of a professional class of Arsenal fans. We moan about prices, but we still end up buying. In a funny way, the moments become more special, the more that access is limited, the more you have to ration yourself. Your memories have a romance to them. But people were taken for granted for too long.

"The one big potential flaw in the whole plan is if Arsenal don't employ proper people, if they don't deliver customer service. We've had price hikes, merchandising, expensive programmes, appalling cups of tea. And growing customer unrest as a result from this growing mass of professional class fans. Loyalty is different now from the sixties and seventies. Loyalty is much more strained by a scenario of poor service. So Arsenal has to get this right, rather than relying entirely on the urbane PR skills of the manager.

"Some thinking has been done, more is needed. The club's done well with its image. The shirts look stylish whereas some years previously they've been naff. Wearing the brand now is fine, you feel confidence and pride. They've made that easier to do. But I'm not sure they've thought through the relationship with fans/supporters/customers. All that has changed. How do we describe ourselves or see ourselves? We're fans but customers, investors too."

Ben is Director of the London Design Festival so he takes a professional interest in matters of design and image. But, particularly in London, this is a common background for football fans. Kevin Whitcher, the editor of *The Gooner*, represents the ordinary Arsenal fan through the fanzine that was first published two decades ago.

"Fanzines came about for many reasons – through the music scene at the time, access to cheap photocopiers, hooliganism declining. And also a sense of alienation from the official club although that has actually got worse since the advent of the Premiership and all-seater stadia. A lot of fans have been completely alienated, mainly because they can't afford to watch football any more.

It could get better. The club needs to listen more, for example to supporter groups. We need more lower priced seats, and a proper policy to develop support among the under-16s. They should be able to sit anywhere in the stadium for half price, not just in the family enclosure. We are in danger of losing a whole generation of fans. If they don't develop the habit of watching now, they won't later. The stadium may improve things, as it may put a natural ceiling on ticket prices as well as allowing more people in. Currently Highbury is like a West End club, 'members only'.

Everyone agrees that the new stadium provides an opportunity to redress some of the inequalities of the past. But the days of football as the "working man's game" are gone and they will not return. Society has moved on and made that impossible. Arsenal has to cater for the customer base it has now and will have in the future. A small sign of change is that the new stadium is being designed with toilets in a 70/30% male/female split (compared with Highbury's recently upgraded 75/25% split). Women will become an increasingly important category of the football audience, and their presence will change things in many ways. Standards of customer service will improve as a result, and that will benefit everyone attending a match. No doubt the atmosphere at matches will change a little too, some will argue for the better.

The other big influence of women on Arsenal's future will also be on the pitch itself. Women's football could be the fastest growing area of the game. It is now becoming a serious sport, and an attractive spectator sport. Compared with ten years ago, women's football is played with much higher levels of skill, speed and athleticism. In ten years' time, given the current rate of development, women's football could be attracting large crowds. Here Arsenal are well-placed, having supported a women's team from its early days of pure amateurism (and the team is still quaintly known as Arsenal Ladies). The women who wear the Arsenal shirt, as the increasing

TV audience will have seen, play the game in a way that is becoming closer to the men's game. Their development has shown in the number of trophies won: seven Premier League titles in 12 years, eight League Cups, six FA Cups. Arsenal dominate the women's game in an increasingly competitive environment. Arsenal have been the main force in creating and growing a new market in the UK through women's football.

The challenge for Arsenal is to make progress in every area of its business. The Arsenal brand has to be central to this challenge. The brand can help Arsenal not only to do the obvious – create a good image – but to drive crucial decisions about the way the club operates. We have called this book *Winning Together* because we believe that phrase represents the essence of the Arsenal brand. Of course, as will all brand statements, it contains a large element of aspiration. Sometimes the club will fall below the ideal. But if the idea of winning together is interpreted with a full understanding of its potential meaning, it will become more than a standard football platitude. The only way for Arsenal to truly win is to win together, and that means engaging the hearts, minds, energy and loyalty of everyone involved in Arsenal, particularly the fans or customers. So it has to look at branding and marketing as disciplines that go beyond the commercial need to maximise revenues. Arsenal must develop marketing plans that continue to generate income while building the love and admiration of a wider circle of audiences. By engaging with fans, by seeing fans as more than just ticket holders, partnerships can be formed and fresh ideas released. The local community, children, women, those disenfranchised by current financial policies, need to be addressed as part of a sustained brand programme, not as boxes to be ticked in a corporate and social responsibility report.

We believe this is achievable and this will be done. In doing so, the ripples will spread not just through domestic audiences but through the international markets that are undoubtedly in the sights of the Arsenal management.

SIX LESSONS IF THE ARSENAL BRAND IS TO WIN

1 Nothing matters more than success on the pitch – the core product drives the brand

2 Concentrate on building the relationship with fans and local community

3 Keeping Arsenal's place as the leader in London football will do more for the brand internationally than any number of pre-season tours of 'target markets'

4 A deeper commitment to customer service is crucial

5 Women and children need to be integrated fully into the life of the brand

6 Build the spirit and links between Arsenal and all its stakeholders – go beyond 'keep informed' to 'get involved'

HIGHBURY

1913 — 2006

THE FINAL
SALUTE